Plea e re

HELEN M. STEVENS'
WORLD
OF
EMBROIDERY

HELEN M. STEVENS'
WORLD
OF
EMBROIDERY

David & Charles

This book (and particularly Plate 48) is dedicated to the memory of the world before 11 September 2001

A DAVID & CHARLES BOOK

First published in the UK in 2002

Designs Copyright © Helen M. Stevens 2002
Text, photography and layout Copyright © David & Charles 2002

Helen M. Stevens has asserted her right to be identified as author of this work in accordance with the Copyright, Designs and Patents Act, 1988.

A catalogue record for this book is available from the British Library.

ISBN 0 7153 0977 3

Executive Editor Cheryl Brown
Executive Art Editor Ali Myer
Desk Editor Sandra Pruski
Project Editor Linda Clements
Book Designer Lisa Forrester
Photography Nigel Salmon
Printed in Singapore by KHL
David & Charles
Brunel House   Newton Abbot   Devon

◁ *PLATE 1 (cover & page 2)*
Humming-birds and trumpet creeper –
a fantasy of colour and movement
23 x 29.25cm (9 x 11½in)

CONTENTS

HELEN M.
STEVENS

FOREWORD

ong ago and far away (as all the best stories begin) there was a warrior, Brithelm, and his wife, Wulfendatter. They loved each other deeply, just as they loved the Old Gods of their far northern land; Brithelm was a fearless fighter, true to his overlord and Wulfendatter was a good wife, skilled in the womanly arts, especially needlework.

Each summer Brithelm would accompany his overlord on campaign, sailing far over the seas in search of new lands, fresh conquests and rich booty. Each autumn Wulfendatter would await his return, and while away the long summer evenings working a great embroidery telling the story of their happy life together, their courtship above the icy waters of the fjords, their marriage in the sacred shrine of Freya and their home in the rolling hills. Every year when her husband returned, Wulfendatter knew her long golden braids were a little more silver, and Brithelm knew that his beard was a little greyer, until one year he did not return. Autumn turned to an aching, cold winter and before spring could warm her Wulfendatter pulled the great embroidery over her body and drifted away into the arms of the Mother Goddess in her final sleep.

Brithelm had fallen on the field of battle. His death had been honourable and the Valkyries carried his soul away to the great tapestry-decked hall of Valhalla where heroes feast for all eternity in the company of Odin, God of War. But Brithelm missed Wulfendatter and begged the Valkyries to bring her to him – all in vain for only warriors may enter Valhalla. As a boon, however, the Valkyries fetched Wulfendatter's great embroidery and it was hung in the mead hall, its colourful silks and skilled stitching bringing back all his memories until the nostalgia for his lost love was too great to bear. He took down the hanging, threw open the great doors of the hall and stepped outside to cast the embroidery, and his memories, into the void. The door swung shut.

Nobody, having left Valhalla, can regain admission, and hammer as he might against the huge carved lintels he could not return, so wrapping the embroidery around his shoulders for warmth, he set out into the eternal night sky to find his love. And still he searches, through the starry constellations of the Lady's Wain, amid the gauzy light of the Milky Way and the unspun silk of the clouds. Sometimes, to remind him of what he seeks, he hangs the great embroidery in the heavens and the vibrant colours and lively patterns of its folds swathe the sky. Clever men of science call it the Aurora Borealis, some people call it the Northern Lights, but to the far north of Middle-earth, when the old folk look into the ancient west to seek out the home of the lost Gods, it is still Wulfendatter's Embroidery.

Modern fairy tale
based upon Scandinavian mythology

INTRODUCTION

Bid the colours of sunset glow!
Let grace in each gliding thread be hid. . .
Let your skein be long and your silk be fine. . .
And time nor chance shall your work untwine;
But all — like a truth — endure.

Barry Cornwall
English Songs and Other Poems

PLATE 5 ▷

Flowers and embroidery have been associated since time immemorial. The lotus appears in ancient Egyptian textile fragments, immured within the tombs of the Pharaohs. The Sacred Blue Lotus of the Nile was the symbol of rebirth.
9.5 x 9.5cm (3³⁄₄ x 3³⁄₄in)

◁ *PLATE 4*

The world of embroidery knits together strands of inspiration from distant corners of the earth and diverse cultures. The Indian balsam (Impatiens glandulifera) *and lesser periwinkle* (Vinca minor) *grow side by side in my country garden. The former is a 'foreigner' imported into England in 1839 and grown in greenhouses until it escaped into the wild. The latter is a native, in medieval times associated with the pagan rites of passage from this world into the next. Pre-Christian Anglo-Saxon mythology held that the mortal world was bound together by the threads of Wyrd, the 'web of life' which caught in its silk the souls of all living things. In North America certain tribes of native peoples believed that the Great Spirit, Manitou, gave to men the magic of the 'dream catcher', a web which caught the evil of nightmares in its snare, letting only sweet dreams and benevolent forces through to the sleeper. Traditionally, dream catchers are decorated with feathers, beads and other trinkets. Observation and imagination together bring this study to life.*
Embroidery shown life-size:
40 x 26.75cm (15³⁄₄ x 10¹⁄₂in)

At the dawn of the twenty-first century our planet is still a place of infinite diversity. From the polar caps to the sultry heat of the tropics, flora, fauna, birds and insects suggest breathtaking inspirational possibilities for embroiderers, whilst the global village which the world has become is held together by the threads of the Internet, video communications and satellite technology. The design concepts, source material and research facilities at our fingertips in the first decade of the new millennium surpass the wildest dreams of artists and embroiderers from past generations.

Working in a textile medium today is a voyage of discovery – a journey through every aspect of modern life in a world influenced by the past, challenged by the present and inspired by the promise of the future. Creativity can be harvested from the environment, the cultural traditions of widely differing civilizations, the heights of the world's literary heritage and the depths of human imagination. It can also be an intensely personal experience. To interpret the world around us we have the ability now to harness the knowledge of eras ancient and modern, inspired by art forms as primitive as Neolithic wall paintings and as advanced as holograms and laser displays.

As this book is published, I celebrate twenty-one years working in my own 'world of embroidery' – over two decades in which textile art has taken many steps forward into mainstream acceptance, or, perhaps more accurately, has begun to re-assume its once pre-eminent place at the apex of applied art. *Opus Anglicanum*, 'English Work', from the Anglo-Saxon era to the Middle Ages, proclaimed its importance by the very simplicity of its name; now embroidery has many meanings from the calming, rhythmic application of counted thread stitches to the thought-provoking, often startling, effects achieved by machine embroidery. Crucially, however, we must never forget that the definition of embroidery is the decoration of an existing fabric by the application of other threads. This can be augmented by the addition of other decorative elements and enhanced by the choice of the background fabric, but ultimately it is the stitch itself which speaks. The variety of its language is infinite, echoing from the distant past or whispering of a far future. How we choose to interpret its voice in the present is our challenge.

Traditionally, the natural world of flowers and foliage, birds, butterflies and animals has gone hand-in-hand with embroidery. In my recent books, *Helen M. Stevens' Embroidered Flowers* and *Helen M. Stevens' Embroidered Butterflies*, I have explored in practical terms how these subjects can be captured in lifelike techniques. The turning cycle of the seasons, reflected in the sheen of sleave silk, the sparkle of sunlight and frost emphasized by fine metallic threads, the mat glow of pure cottons, are effects which have evolved through centuries of embroidered

◁ *PLATE 6*
Split stitch, one of the earliest recognizable
filling techniques in European embroidery, is
used here to create the 'jigsaw' effect of colour
surrounding surface-couched goldwork in a
reconstruction of early eighth and ninth
century English work. Possibly a motif
combining the symbols for alpha and omega, or
a monogrammed elaboration of the initial 'M'
for the Virgin, this piece would have been
worked on dense evenweave linen, cut out and
hemmed, and applied to more ornate fabric,
such as loom-woven silk. Seed pearls are used to
enhance the outline.
12.75 x 12cm (5 x 4³/₄in)

application from stylized decorative motifs (Plate 6) to descriptive, realistic studies (Plate 7, overleaf).

In the sixteenth century, when the New World began to yield its secrets to an incredulous generation, the fantastic birds and beasts of the newly explored territories soon found their way into embroidery design, from bestiary to bed or wall hangings in one easy step – as Mary Queen of Scots' and Bess of Hardwick's famous tent stitch creations bear eloquent witness (Fig 1). In our own age, the revolutionary breakthroughs in communications, advances in photographic techniques and the determination to record and understand the complexities of life on Earth, continue to reveal new images of breathtaking and sometimes savage beauty.

The natural world presents many enigmas and mysteries. In the deep, 'blue holes' of the great oceans previously unrecorded species are still being discovered and in the shadows of the rain forests the secret lives of many animals and insects are yet to be fully understood. New and unfamiliar plants, as well as exotic favourites such as cacti and orchids, suggest vivid designs and the qualities of modern embroidery are perfect to explore their potential. Just as the elephant and the leopard were once crudely interpreted from naïve woodcut to canvas stitch, so we can now take images from freeze-frame photography to describe in silk and modern fibres the iridescent glow of a humming-bird (Plate 1, jacket cover and page 2), or the flash of a tiger's eye.

Throughout the centuries and across the planet, striking images of their own cultural heritage and beliefs have been created by native peoples and civilizations.

△ *Fig 1*
When the New World began to open up,
inspiration arrived in the shape of bestiaries
suggesting all manner of exciting subjects. A
surprising liveliness is apparent in many
woodcut designs which still make attractive
motifs today.

PLATE 7 ▽

The idea of the ever-changing cycle of the seasons works wonderfully well as an embroidery. Clockwise from the bottom, the flowers from winter through to autumn are winter aconites (Eranthis hyemalis) *and snowdrops* (Galanthus nivalis), *heartsease* (Viola tricolor), *the wild dog rose* (Rosa canina), *white bryony* (Bryonia dioica), *traveller's-joy* (Clematis vitalba), *holly* (Ilex aquifolium) *and ivy* (Hedera helix). *The field mouse eyes the best berries, just out of his reach, lightly resting a paw on a snowdrop bud.*
22.25 x 22.25cm (8³/₄ x 8³/₄in)

Textiles, woven, embellished and embroidered, have formed a rich and enduring reservoir of information about these sometimes lost, sometimes flourishing worlds. Embroidery can capture and recreate these concepts and images in many ways – both by interpreting the styles and techniques of their countries of origin and by using the ideas themselves in familiar ways. To the indigenous North American tribes the imagery of feathers and cobwebs combined in the creation of the 'dream-catcher' (Plates 4 and 8). We can invest their ideas with our own input to expand and elaborate, or condense and miniaturize. The Taj Mahal has become a timeless tribute to romantic love (Plate 32, page 60, detail Plate 9) and we can use the beauty of its architecture to explore new dimensions of embroidery – cool, watery reflections and dusty pathways through the heat of the Indian sub-continent.

Children never tire of hearing a favourite fairy tale time and time again. In adult life, novels, poems, plays and music are all responses to the eternal demand for

entertainment – fundamentally they are telling us stories. Embroidery, too, can be (indeed, always has been) a narrative tool. The textile images found in Viking ship burials, like the wall paintings in a Pharaoh's tomb, stride across their canvas in a bold strip-cartoon of action. The embroidered hangings of the Middle Ages and the great tapestries of the Renaissance told stories of contemporary events and re-told the tales of antiquity. Modern embroideries need be no less diverse or expressive. The images of a happy childhood, memories of places loved and explored, and youthful adventures shared, may be conjured up through the magic of broad, sweeping landscape techniques and minute, delicate stitching (Plate 10 and detail Plate 63, page 109). Combinations of bold, impressionistic swathes of colour and fine, intimate detail are the true embroiderer's passport to expressing their own narrative reality in a uniquely expressive medium.

In order to believe something fantastic, it is often only necessary to 'suspend disbelief'. Worlds created by the imagination, Shangri-La, Middle-earth, Gormenghast, open the doors of our minds to new and amazing vistas. In places such as these there need be no constraint other than the limits of our inspiration. As we enter the age of Aquarius and space flight becomes a reality, the exploration of worlds other than our own is a real possibility. With the materials and tools now at the disposal of embroiderers, extraterrestrial ideas, the minutiae of 'inner space' and whole new mind-sets can be created in shimmering, translucent, three-dimensional effects. In the final chapters of this book, by experimenting and pushing the boundaries of embroidery toward new goals – whilst still retaining the essential and ancient elements of the art – we take a leap of faith into the future, though keeping a firm footing in tradition.

Helen M. Stevens' World of Embroidery is perhaps the most personal book I have ever created – a collection of pictures which reflect the world as I see it through

△ *Fig 2*
A simple study of flowers from your own garden can suggest inter-continental travel. Here the familiar common field poppy (Papaver rhoeas) *right, blooms alongside the Californian poppy* (Eschscholzia californica).

◁ *PLATE 8*
A tiny embroidery can sometimes capture the same drama as a large piece, if every element is chosen carefully. A short frond of rosebay willow-herb (Epilobium angustifolium) *suspends a delicate spider's web and its builder, whilst a mayfly* (Ephemera danica) *dances close by. Colours have been emphasized to give impact to this miniature study – the blue-green wings of the mayfly and deep pink of the flower are also slightly simplified to give greater impact. Compare this picture with Plate 4 – size does not always matter!*
8.25 x 7cm (3½ x 2¾in)

PLATE 10 *(far right)* ▷

'As I stepped out one May morning. . .' Laurie Lee's descriptions of his West Country home paint pictures in the mind of endless springs and summers and the freedom of childhood. This picture was commissioned to evoke memories of a Lincolnshire childhood – the rolling Wolds, stag-antlered oak trees and fields sporting the once almost universal swathes of poppies and daisies.

The little owl (Athene noctua) *was introduced into Britain in the nineteenth century from continental Europe. By early in the twentieth century it had colonized most of England and Wales. Territorial birds, the adults adopt favourite perches – often certain fence posts or tree stumps are regarded as private property – from which they make forays in search of molluscs, worms and insects, and an occasional very small mammal.*

40.5 x 29cm (16 x 11½in)

the eye of my own needle. As well as images of familiar subjects (sometimes conveyed in unexpected ways), I have been able to work studies which, over the years, have suggested themselves to me as challenging, innovative and rewarding. My inspiration has come from nature, travel, history, literature and, on occasion, my students and clients – whose queries as to how I might attempt certain obscure projects have often given me pause for thought and the odd very late night!

As in my previous books, I offer these embroideries as inspiration and encouragement to embroiderers and artists in a variety of media. My interpretations may be used as launch-pads for your own voyages into the unknown but, as ever, certain golden rules are valuable anchors in the rough waters of unfamiliar techniques. Whether you are designing from nature or imagination, make sketches which emphasize the primary elements of your picture. Remember that light and shade, observed movement, contrasting and complementary colours, which seem so obvious when inspiration strikes, can be difficult to recall later when accurate and precise drawing is needed to transfer the basic outline from paper to fabric. Make initial notes and jottings which will enable you to recapture those essential effects later (see Figs 3 and 4).

Imaginative and innovative ideas can be incorporated into otherwise naturalistic studies with surprising results. The dormouse in Plate 11, as he clambers

PLATE 9 *(Detail of Plate 32)* ▷

Although the overall majesty of the Taj Mahal is only fully evident in a study of the whole building (Plate 32, page 60) when we explore small sections of the embroidery they can reveal the secrets of a successful rendition. Careful placing of reflections (the trees are mirrored for only a portion of their length) and a blurring of details in the inverted image are subtle interpretations which avoid a 'picture postcard' effect. Don't be afraid to look deeply into the world of technical know-how as well as fanciful inspiration!

Detail shown: 11 x 19cm (4¼ x 7½in)

amongst ruby-red rosehips, is conveyed as accurately as possible – his fuzzy fur is emphasized by outer strata of stitching in progressively finer gauges of silk; his whiskers (cheek, pouch and eyebrow) quiver, overlaid across the underlying stitches; his toes, grasping the branch, are worked in mat cotton to contrast with the shine of his coat. Bringing an element of magic to the piece tiny, uncut semi-precious gems are applied in a chevron to the bottom corner of the motif. Green peridot suggests the upward thrust of foliage, while goldstones bring an earthy element to the lower dimension. Don't be afraid to mix your textures and depths of focus to draw the viewer into a piece.

Just as in nature there is no substitute for observation, so, when designing from the imagination, there is nothing better than new and exciting materials to suggest fresh ideas. When a potential subject presents itself, such as the Northern Lights or scudding starlit clouds (Plate 2 and detail Plate 74, page 122), you may wish to seek out threads to fit a particular purpose. Conversely, an exciting fabric may inspire you to work a wholly amazing design to startling effect. Marbled fabrics or even dull shades can impart dramatic atmospheres to unusual scenes – Queen Mab of Faerie (Plate 70, page 119) and the Jackdaw of Rheims (Plate 53, page 90), respectively, are just such examples.

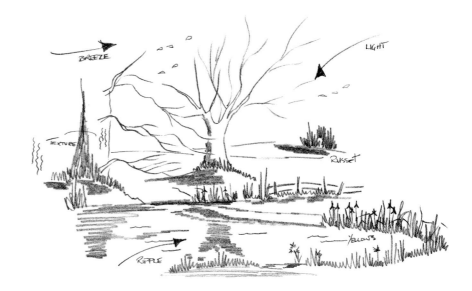

Fig 3 ▷
Get in the habit of jotting down notes to
remind yourself of vital aspects of a scene.

Unusual subjects sometimes call for unexpected presentation. Naturally, the addition of stones and beads necessitates the use of a deep mount to keep glass away from the materials but other more imaginative ideas can also enhance your work. Double mounting, or creating a mount or window which is itself embroidered, changes the dimensions of a piece. Inspiration for framing elements within the

PLATE 11 ▷

The common dormouse (Muscardinus avallanarius) *can live up to six years, though much of its life in Britain is spent alone and asleep, as it hibernates from October to April. In late summer and autumn body weight is built up by eating hazel nuts, hips, haws and other seasonal foods in preparation for the long winter sleep, during which the dormouse curls itself into a small furry parcel, tail wrapped around its head and paws clenched beneath its chin (see bottom of Plate 77, page 128). Viewing an animal 'full frontal' as opposed to in part or full profile allows us to explore the use of radial* opus plumarium *to its greatest effect. With the 'core' of the study formed by the nose of the subject, it is easy to understand the principle of all the stitches falling back towards the all-important growing point. This basic rule applies to most creatures, from the familiar to the more exotic.*
10 x 10cm (4 x 4in)

◁ *Fig 4*
Something about this lovely country cottage
made me smile! It had a definite 'face' and
looked as though it was chuckling about some
private joke. Just in case I forgot that
atmosphere I gave myself a reminder –
'Happy' Cottage.

overall design, allowing a simpler actual frame, can also emphasize the textural quality of the work. These may be drawn from many sources: interior decoration, fashion accessories and, of course, the natural world. The ultimate display of the finished piece also has a bearing upon its success. Lighting, for instance, both natural and artificial, should be considered when choosing an ultimate home for your embroideries. All these aspects of the embroiderer's art are discussed.

The final sections of this book deal with other practicalities. The pages concerning stitches and techniques (Appendices A and B) have been updated from previous titles in this series to take account of their ever-widening applications. Whilst I am aware that many readers enjoy both text and illustrations on a purely aesthetic level, I know that many also appreciate a more practical approach. I hope that these sections continue to be both informative and helpful.

My *World of Embroidery* is a place of limitless horizons where pleasure, relaxation and entertainment form a heady mix with challenge, inspiration and experimentation. I invite you in, and offer this collection as a gateway to your own journeys of exploration and flights of fancy. Let your imagination, and your needle, take wing.

◁ *Fig 5*
Very distinctive stitch flow directions will be
used in the embroidery which results from this
preliminary sketch – spiralling, perpendicular
and horizontal (see Plate 66, page 112).
Choosing a correctly lit 'home' for your
completed work is important.

CHAPTER ONE

SEA FEVER

Soft soft wind, from out of the sweet south sliding,
Waft thy silver cloud-webs athwart the summer sea;
Thin thin threads of mist on dewy fingers twining
Weave a veil of dappled gauze to shade my babe and me.

Charles Kingsley
The Water Babies

THE RUNNING TIDE

PLATE 13 ▷

Most people are more familiar with the family of the Hottentot fig in its guise as the ever-popular Livingstone daisy (Mesembryanthemum)*, a garden favourite – though only when it opens in sunny weather. In a dull summer its colourful flowers remain stubbornly closed and its glistening, succulent leaves dull and bland. In bright, warm conditions, however, it is a spectacular plant, thriving in sandy soil – hence its success as a naturalized escapee in coastal areas of the West Country of England.*
9.5 x 10cm (3¾ x 4in)

◁ *PLATE 12*

It's a beautiful but tough world if you're a baby cod (Gadus morhua)*. Tempted by the shimmering, waving tips of a jellyfish's tentacles, you could become its victim; swim to the sea floor among pebbles and shellfish and you might fall prey to ever-vigilant dogfish. As many as nine million eggs may hatch into fry from a single female, so despite natural predators there should be plenty of cod to maintain one of the oldest fishing industries – but even so stocks are becoming depleted. In an underwater world we can abandon many concepts which, in our own environment, might overwork a picture. While the codling bodies are worked in receding strata of* opus plumarium, *their elongated, almost transparent fins are lent sparkle by fine silver metallic thread, and the whole overlaid in places by extended straight stitches in cellophane thread. To add to the three-dimensional qualities effected by building up layers of stitching, other features are allowed to stand proud of the surface embroidery: the thread weeds (left and centre) are created by floating embroidery (see text) and the sea floor is scattered with tiny real shells.*
Embroidery shown life-size:
41.25 x 25.5cm (16¼ x 10in)

From the black velvet vastness of outer space our planet appears to spin through the universe like a small blue and white sequin, crowned and tipped at the poles by ice and snow, swathed by skeins of diaphanous cloud, but chiefly catching and reflecting its sun's rays in the depths of its blue-green waters.

The majority of the Earth's surface is covered with water: it is the cradle of life and, at its deepest, as mysterious and unexplored as the heavens. Where the sea meets the shore there is a magical dimension in which two worlds mingle. As we stroll on the broad sweep of a sandy beach and explore the tide's litter of flotsam and jetsam, or stand on a high cliff watching the circling sea birds and the distant play of the ocean's animal life, new vistas open in the imagination.

It is impossible to say who first stepped into the unknown and launched a craft into the waves. Perhaps famine made a people desperate enough to leave dry land and seek out new homes; perhaps mankind's inherent wanderlust was always too strong to be denied, but since pre-history races have sent first warriors and explorers, then settlers and migrants across treacherous waters to seek their fortunes and bring them back to the old country, or set up new colonies and ultimately new homes. As diverse civilizations met each other for the first time, recorded history began to unfold; sea journeys were often the catalysts which set these sequences in motion.

It was natural for alien cultures, unfamiliar habitats and the extraordinary creatures and plants of the oceans to be greeted with astonishment by the voyagers. Flora and fauna needed names to which newcomers could relate – folk names for everyday use and later scientific classification for the scholars. Through the names which have been afforded to some sea and shore life we can effect an entry into the interpretation of many of these wonderful subjects. Plate 12 brings together a pretty combination of names, curiosities and design concepts.

Sailors were once notoriously superstitious, not surprising, given that the uncontrollable elements of wind and water held their lives hanging by a thread – the gods and lesser deities had to be appeased and ill fortune avoided at all costs. A belief in strange sea creatures was universal and, to the minds of ancient seafarers, proof positive of the existence of monsters, sea sprites and mermaids was all around – surely the underwater 'fire' of jellyfish and other phosphorescent animals was evidence of magical forces at work; the 'purses' washed up at high tide the property of mermaids and mermen? Certainly the papery egg capsules of the lesser spotted dogfish (*Scyliorhinus canicula*), found dried out along the shore-line with their long, drawstring tendrils had every appearance of desiccated silk – if they were always empty of treasures it was because they were invariably ripped open! Bottom right in Plate 12, a 'mermaid's purse' is anchored to the waving frond of dulse (*Palmaria palmata*). Several inches long, the 'purse' remains intact for up to eleven months while the young dogfish develops, and is finally torn open as the pup emerges (Fig 6). The discarded, tattered sac is then dislodged by the tides, free to be deposited along a beach with the other debris of the sea. The pearl jellyfish (*Pelagia noctiluca*) similarly provided evidence of mysterious sea dwellers. Dark and dormant when undisturbed, it fluoresces when touched (and can impart a painful sting) leaving traces of glowing light on anything it brushes. Removed from the water its magic is extinguished – its pale pink pearls only weave their spells for inhabitants of its own environment.

Both the dome of the jellyfish's umbrella and the silky sac of the mermaid's purse can be worked in the simplest of decorative techniques – basic straight and filling stitches and applied thread in the shape of surface couching. The outlines of the jellyfish's body and the belly and tendrils of the purse are defined by surface couched blending filament and gold thread respectively, infilled with lightly angled *opus plumarium*. On the former, the stitching is left 'open' to allow the background fabric to show between the filaments and create a translucent effect; on the latter, changing shades and voiding suggests the contours of the inner yolk sac. Whilst these techniques appear complex at first glance, they are only extensions and adaptations of skills which are applied throughout this collection of embroideries. The feathery tentacles of the pearl jellyfish are worked in a further evolution of directional *opus plumarium*, with the slender arms in snake stitch. These two techniques are most simply explained by reference to the long fronds of the mermaid's tresses (*Chorda filum*), an elegant seaweed of the lower shore.

Where the long arc of a motif sweeps only in one direction, it can be described by a single swathe of simple snake stitch, but where it changes direction, the flow of the stitches would be interrupted; in these cases reflexing snake stitch should be used (Fig 7). An extended, single stratum of radial *opus plumarium*, with a change of colour depth to

◁ *Fig 6*
Tiny dogfish emerge from the 'mermaids' purses' leaving them tattered, though often still attached to their anchoring plant. Eventually they are shaken free by the tide and washed up on the beach – mysterious remnants of the sea's diversity.

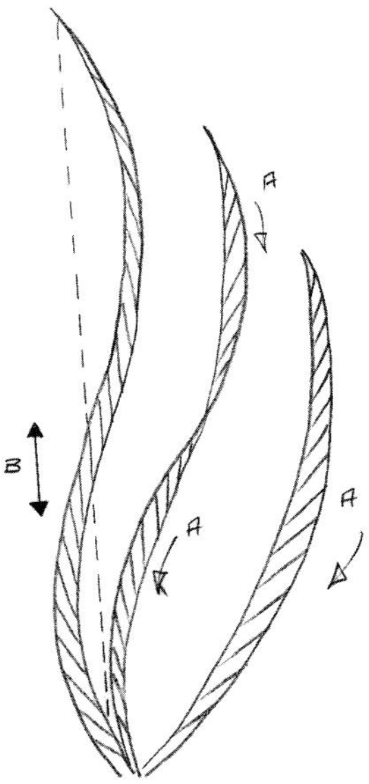

◁ *Fig 7*
Simple snake stitch (right, A) takes the form of a narrow arc of directional opus plumarium; *two opposing angles of stitching create the impression of a single frond with a twist (centre, A). To the left, reflexing snake stitch creates a sinuous curve: determine the direction of stitching (B) by taking a line mid-way between the tip and base of the motif, then stitch upward to the tip, and downward to the base, always remembering the 'out on the outside and in on the inside' rule of stitching.*

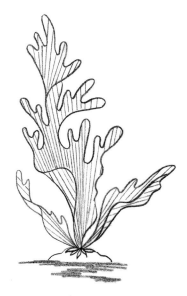

△ *Fig 8*

Even a deeply serrated motif such as the dulse
seaweed can be worked in simple radial opus
plumarium *if the rule of opposite angle*
stitching for the reflexed fields of the design are
well observed.

suggest the underside of the motif (worked in opposite angle stitching), performs the same task on the dulse (Fig 8).

Appropriately, the dogfish itself is worked in Dalmatian dog technique. The deep chocolate-brown spots which give the fish its name are stitched first, with successive strata of *opus plumarium* flooded around them. Outlined in gold and silver surface couched metallic thread, a smooth, slippery contour is effected.

Added movement is created by the addition of fine details such as bubbles, ripples and swirls in the 'water' and by the waving, free-flowing lines of the ceramium, or thread, seaweed. These are worked in floating embroidery, a technique which, coincidentally, I first developed having encountered a tangled mass of traveller's-joy (*Clematis vitalba*) in a north Cornish hedgerow whilst returning from a sea-side walk (see Plate 14). The stitch lends itself well to any motif which needs to appear unfettered to the background fabric (see Appendix A, page 129).

The contrast between Plates 13 and 14 perfectly encapsulates the qualities which make embroidery such a unique medium. In Plate 13 the Hottentot fig (*Carpobrotus edulis*), a native of south-west Africa, now naturalized near the sea in England in Cornwall and Devon, is a fleshy, trailing plant, bearing upward-curving leaves, triangular in cross-section. The many-petalled flowers are yellow and magenta, and the whole dense plant glistens with a sugary glaze of transparent cells. Close, full-bodied stitching, overlaid with a touch of cellophane thread and the design bounded by short, straight-stitched grasses, defines the prostrate, sprawling habit of the species. Plate 14 is entirely dissimilar. Airy and open, the feathery seed-heads of the clematis invite the eye to look through the stitching to the cores within. These cap long, slender stems − worked in reflexing and graduating stem stitch − sporting delicate tendrils and fine leaves. The same silk has been used to create both pictures: by employing different gauges, plies and tensions, it describes both to perfection.

NOW VOYAGER

Ancient Greek seafarers, when they first encountered the fascinating little sea-horse (*Sygnathisformes*), believed that it was a chimera − a strange and magical mixture of animals with the head of a horse, the lungs of a fish, the tail of a monkey and a chameleon's ability to change colour. Not surprisingly, they ascribed to it supernatural properties − live, sea-horses carried messages to the sea gods; dead, they imparted a powerful poison when soaked in wine, though their ashes mixed with honey and vinegar was an antidote to other lethal potions. Pliny, the Roman scholar, recommended powdered sea-horse as a cure for baldness, skin eruptions and the bite of mad dogs! Even in the ancient world, the sea-horse's hold on survival was tentative.

Sea-horses are monogamous and each bonded pair produce thousands of young, but on average only two offspring survive their parents. One of the sea's slowest moving life forms − they rarely travel above 0.01 miles per hour

◁ *PLATE 14*

*Presented in a deep frame, the glass held well
away from the work by a window mount, the
three-dimensional qualities of floating
embroidery are seen here to best advantage.
By lighting the piece thoughtfully – from
a slight angle – the shadow of the looped
stitches is thrown across the background fabric
creating a superb natural effect. By interlacing
the elegantly curving stems of the plant this
impression is further emphasized. Though it is
often fun to create elaborate, multi-faceted
designs (such as Plate 12) a simple,
beautifully crafted piece such as this – there are
only five colours used throughout – can be
equally satisfying.*

13 x 23cm (5 x 9in)

(0.016kmph) – they are prey to tuna, skates, rays, crabs and other predators, and those that escape natural hunters often fall victim to man, not only for supposed medicinal purposes (some cultures still believe Pliny!) but as tourist souvenirs. In South-east Asia up to eight million sea-horses may be killed in a single year, many only to be dried and used as key fobs or pencil tops.

A better way to enjoy the ethereal beauty of this lovely little animal is to recreate it in embroidery (Plate 15). One of nature's anomalies, the sea-horse is actually a fish, but without scales or many of the other features with which fish are usual identified. Its body, covered by a suit of tough 'armour' plates, is propelled along vertically – and very slowly – by a single tiny fin on its back, which moves so quickly that it is virtually invisible. The challenge in embroidery is to suggest its spiny, rigid outer shell, whilst retaining a feeling of frailty. As with many underwater subjects, fine metallic gold and silver threads come to our rescue. Initially, the segments of armour are worked in silk, without attempting an overall directional sweep, keeping each section separate and voiding between each. The gills on the head are suggested by several narrow sweeps of single-stranded silver thread, and the eye, worked with a black pupil and a minute 360 degree circle of radial *opus*

PLATE 15 ▷

At the mercy of the sea's currents, the sea-horse tries to remain anchored to a safe haven in the shape of seaweed or fine coral. To maintain its upright position a buoyancy balloon must be kept fully inflated – if one bubble of gas escapes the sea-horse sinks to the ocean floor where it must await a sufficient build up of gas to re-inflate its tank.

To create the realistic effect of one element coiling around another, sketch a simplified version of the motif (Fig 10). Remember the 'in front/behind' principle of all interlaced subjects, and if two or more fronds are woven into the equation (as here), decide which is your primary subject. In this instance the tail of the sea-horse goes in front x 1 (tip of the tail), behind x 2 (central seaweed frond) and in front x 2 (right-hand seaweed frond). It may sound complicated, but it works!

9.5 x 10cm (3³⁄₄ x 4in)

plumarium, is highlighted with a seed stitch in white. Then, between and around each segment of the body a thicker gold or silver thread is applied, surface couched to fill the waiting voids and outline the contour of the fish (Fig 9). The sea-horse's ability to camouflage itself by changing colour to imitate its surroundings means that you have a wide choice of colourways. Here, I have chosen a pale green-gold silk toward the dorsal surface, blending to silver below.

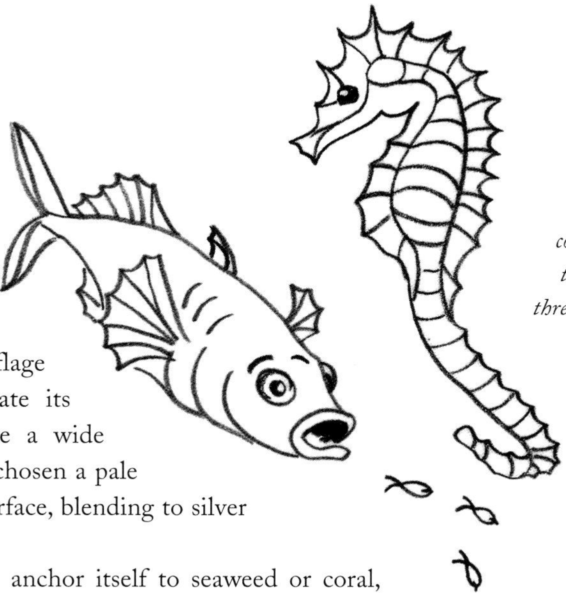

◁ Fig 9
Simplified aquatic designs are perfect for the use of surface couching to pick out outlines and contours within the motif. Both the sea-horse and the stickleback (left) could be worked in directional stitching and then highlighted by gold or silver metallic threads around each of the lines given. The tiny water 'fleas' are worked in a single lazy daisy stitch augmented by a tiny straight stitched 'V' (see text).

The sea-horse uses its tail to anchor itself to seaweed or coral, feeding upon passing animal plankton. These tiny scraps of water life can be suggested by a simple but very effective motif: using the finest available thread work a minute 'lazy daisy' stitch body, followed by a horizontal 'V' in straight stitch to create a tail. A trail of these wisps leads the eye through the seaweed to the sea-horse's muzzle. In this study, thread-weeds are worked in graduating and reflexing stem stitch, shades of colour blending from a silver-mauve into silver-green. Bubbles and swirls of translucent water effects complete the picture.

Like the Greeks and many other great cultures before them, the English nation reached a golden age of sea-borne exploration, and exploitation of the oceans for hunting, trade, colonisation and warfare followed. The tradition of rendering ships in embroidery is ancient indeed. It is recorded that Helen of Troy embroidered a huge curtain showing the flotilla launched as a precursor to the Trojan Wars. Remnants of textiles bearing ship motifs are found in Viking ship burials and Saxon wall hangings, and the Bayeux Tapestry is a valuable historic document detailing the warships of the eleventh century (Fig 11). In the twentieth century, naval exploits during the Second World War are recorded in the 'Overlord' tapestry, bringing the tradition right up to date. With such a vast range of alternatives, it can only be a matter of personal preference as to our embarkation upon the embroidery of ships. I have chosen to include here a portrait of Henry VIII's famous warship, the *Mary Rose* (Plate 16).

All great ships have a special majesty, but some subjects seem better suited to interpretation than others – rigging, streaming pennants, flags, bunting and the ornate decoration so beloved of the Tudors makes the *Mary Rose* a marvellous study. By working from source material of the period, the 'Anthony Roll', showing a contemporary illustration of the ship produced by the Board of Ordnance in the Tower of London in 1536, we can not only enjoy a marvellous and detailed design, but also try to tailor our work to imitate some of the artistic influences of the day.

Typical of Tudor illustrations of this period, the perspective of the ship is a little skewed. Whilst we see the prow of the ship in profile, the stern appears almost

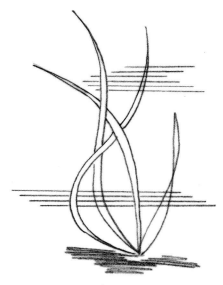

△ Fig 10
Interlacing both primary design and setting gives a three-dimensional effect. Here, the three main fronds each pass 'before and behind' each other, whilst the parallel stitches, which suggest the water, echo the arrangement.

HELEN
STEVENS

PLATE 16
In 1982 I was commissioned to work a limited
edition of embroideries in aid of the fund-
raising projects connected with the raising of
the Mary Rose _from the sea-bed of the Solent_
on the south coast of England. Working from
the historical data available, and the only
extant illustration of the ship, was a
fascinating project – though after working
several versions of the edition I began to
fantasize about sinking it myself! Over a mile
of pure silk was included in each study and
about 2,300 stitches were needed for the guns
alone. Ultimately, the completed issue was of
ten embroideries which have exchanged hands
world-wide.
39.25 x 27.25cm (15^{1}/$_{2}$ x 10^{3}/$_{4}$in)

Fig 11 ▷
Most of the ships in the Bayeux Tapestry are so
full of foot-soldiers that it is hard to see their
structure when under sail. 'Disembark' the
passengers and we can see one man on the tiller
and another taking charge of the rigging.

to face us – the bristling armament of cannons jut out from gun-ports at every conceivable angle while the flags flutter in unconvincingly perfect union. The overall effect, however, is of power and authority – the elements of stylization serving to emphasize the solidity of the subject. I have tried to tailor my stitches to the same effect.

Each deck of the ship is worked in an independent sweep of directional *opus plumarium*, voided to allow the later addition of the other features. These are worked in straight stitching, naïve (and again slightly out of perspective) areas of radial work on the cannons, overlaid and shooting stitches on the flags. Turning to the masts and the rigging, lines have been kept as straight and clean as possible, to contrast with the fluid snake stitching and directional *opus plumarium* of the long pennants. Each rope in the rigging is described by a single long stitch, uncouched, in places passing across the underlying features.

Whatever subject you choose to interpret, remember that a ship needs a sea in which to float! Waters appear to darken as they fall beneath the shadow of other features, so deeper shades applied close to the base of the ship gradually lighten as they emerge from its shade. 'White horses' are suggested by areas of white silk within the overall horizontally straight stitched water, and where the anchor rope disappears, a ripple, also in white, and emphasized by a darker shade, forms in an ellipse. Further exploration of water and reflections are to be found in later chapters.

TRADE WINDS, FUR AND FEATHER

As mankind's supremacy over the waters increased, so the oceans increasingly fell prey to his avarice. Where native peoples once took harvest from the sea to sustain their own needs, migrant trappers and hunters began to exploit its animals for export; fur traders and settlers waged war against natural predators which threatened their stock and livelihoods.

The Esquimaux and Inuit tribes of the far north, together with other inhabitants of the icy wastes, had always trapped animals for food and furs. No part of the beast was wasted: meat was eaten fresh or salted, fat and blubber rendered

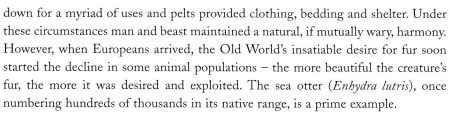

◁ *Fig 12*
Ship, viaduct or distant cliff – all need to be balanced by their reflections. Take a little time to establish where the deepest shadows are thrown and work those first, allowing the more diffuse effect of the reflected elements to emerge gradually.

down for a myriad of uses and pelts provided clothing, bedding and shelter. Under these circumstances man and beast maintained a natural, if mutually wary, harmony. However, when Europeans arrived, the Old World's insatiable desire for fur soon started the decline in some animal populations – the more beautiful the creature's fur, the more it was desired and exploited. The sea otter (*Enhydra lutris*), once numbering hundreds of thousands in its native range, is a prime example.

Whilst the use of sea otter pelts is recorded as part of the textile finery of Russia's infamous Ivan the Terrible (d.1560), its brush with extinction truly begins in the early eighteenth century when the Chinese mandarins were introduced to the fur. They were willing to pay vast sums for embroidered robes trimmed with sea otter pelt or whole gowns worked in its rich golden-brown knap. By 1874 Capt. Charles Scammon of the U.S. Revenue Service (now the U.S. Coastguard) wrote, 'The most valuable fur-bearing animals. . . of the North-western coast of North America are the Sea Otters'. At the turn of the century a single pelt was realizing $1,000 and by 1910 only twenty-four skins reached the European market – so few sea otters were left from their original population that they were hardly worth pursuing. The following year all hunting of seas otters on the 'high seas' was banned by international agreement.

The properties which made the sea otter's fur so desirable also make it a wonderful subject for embroidery (see Plate 17, detail of Plate 60, page 102). Its habits and characteristics are equally enchanting. Spending most of their lives in the water, the thick inner layer of fur has evolved to be an efficient 'wet suit' keeping the icy water away from the animal's body. Constant grooming keeps it in condition whilst an outer layer of longer, glistening hairs traps air to further insulate the skin. Long, wiry whiskers are sensitive to touch and vibration, shorter fur on the paws make them effective in handling food and 'cuddling' their young which often rest on their parent's belly or float alongside wrapped in a fond embrace. To create a successful full-faced study, careful use of radial *opus plumarium* and subdued voiding detail the features whilst softening potentially hard outlines.

▽ *Fig 13*
The adult grey seal (Halichoerus grypus) *has a smooth water-resistant coat that allows it to spend most of its time in icy waters. Dalmatian dog spotting and smooth radial* opus plumarium *are the techniques which would best capture these qualities. The young seal has a dense, fluffy coat to protect it from the cold. Radial work should be overlaid with softening stitches to subdue any stark voids.*

Always work specific facial features first. Here, the nose is worked in mat cotton to contrast with the sheen of the 'fur' and the eyes in floss silk, opposite-angled – again to present a contrast – this time in the directional stitching. As with all radial work, complete the inner strata first (muzzle, cheek pouches, chin, etc.), moving straight into second and third strata where there is no break in perspective, but voiding between specific features, such as beneath the mouth, jawline and above the 'stop' at the forehead. The mother is bobbing almost upright in the water, her lower body dipping below the surface in a downward flow of stitches. The baby, however, is floating more on its back and its tummy fur is therefore at a different angle, fanning upward. Before beginning a study such as this analyze the various elements of the subject and make a 'shorthand' sketch to remind yourself of the directional sweeps to help you with the interpretation (Fig 13). When the basic structure of the animal is complete, subdue the voiding by overlaying fine stitches from one element to the next, always taking your stitches from the 'nearer' feature into the further. Finally, highlight the eyes with white seed stitches and in the same technique create the black 'freckles' on the cheek pouches, from which long straight stitched whiskers can overlay all the underlying work.

The water is worked in two textures of pure silk – untwisted floss where the surface is broken into ripples by the movement of the animals, and a fine, twisted thread where broader areas open out into the wider canvas of the whole embroidery

PLATE 17 (Detail of Plate 60) ▷
In his book Ring of Bright Water *(1959)*
Gavin Maxwell described the joy of living
with otters. Both river and sea otters are
enchanting creatures, playful, affectionate and
graceful and a joy for artists in all media.
The indigenous Aleut peoples of Alaska carried
amulets in the shape of otters and their
pups (see Fig 14).
Working in fine silk allows more than one
shade to be used in the needle at the same time.
Here, gold, brown, pale and dark grey and
white are all variously combined to create
diverse blends of colour, light and shadow.
See also Plate 60.
Detail shown: 11.5 x 9.5cm (4¼ x 3¾in)

(see Plate 60). This plied silk works equally well to suggest close-ups or distant stretches of water such as the estuary in Plate 18. Whilst the waters of the loch or shore in this picture only cover a small percentage of the background it is still a dominant feature of the study, setting the scene for the action above.

The magnificent osprey (*Pandion haliaetus*) once enjoyed an almost world-wide distribution; it could find a home anywhere that deep inshore waters supported a thriving fish population, but again, the encroachment of man upon its natural habitats has, in many places, made the osprey rare. In many populated areas its decline has been spectacular, partly because it vied with man for fish and partly sharing (unjustly) the prejudice which many farmers held against eagles generally, believing they threatened young lambs and other stock. In the nineteenth century a thriving trade existed in osprey eggs and feathers, the former becoming more sought after as they became rarer. Happily now, even in areas of Britain in which it was almost extinct, the osprey is beginning a long, slow come-back.

An osprey making a kill is a dramatic sight, with fish making up most of its diet. The bird hawks high over the water until it spots a fish close to the surface, then it stoops with half-closed wings, entering the water feet first and sending up a great spume of spray, often submerging completely for a few seconds. After a successful dive, it surfaces with a fish in its talons, pauses in mid flight to shake the water from its feathers and then carries its prey back to the nest. Like the sea otter's fur, the feathers of the osprey protect its body from the cold waters of its victim's environment. Unlike the otter, however, there is no soft, fuzzy element to this subject: the ruthless beauty of the sea eagle is stark and sharply defined.

Although the shadow line is important in all studies on a pale background, here it is particularly vital, not only to outline the underside of the bird, but also to define the edges of large, strategic feathers and give substance to the otherwise soft contours of the underbelly and upper legs. As ever, the shadow line should be worked first, always keeping in mind the imagined light source within your picture, using fine stem stitch where a smooth edge is needed, and fragmented straight stitches where the outline is less defined (such as on the backward-facing contours of the 'pantaloons'). Once this is complete, the infill of the body, wings and so on, can be effected, treating the tip of the beak as the core towards which all the radiating stitches will fall.

Smooth strata of radial *opus plumarium* describe the head, neck and body, changing shade and colour where necessary, but without breaking ranks in the stitching, branching off at the pivot point of shoulder (to open out into the inner wing) and thighs (sweeping down into the legs). The long primary feathers of the wing are treated like elongated 'leaves', a single straight stitch forming the quill at the centre of each feather, directional *opus plumarium* worked along each side. These are followed, respectively, by the secondary and smaller feathers, finally merging into the inner wing, where the join is disguised and subdued by shooting long straight stitches from the latter across abutting strata. This order of working is set out in Fig 15 and see also Plate 19. Barring on the wing is overlaid in straight stitching, the smaller markings in ticking.

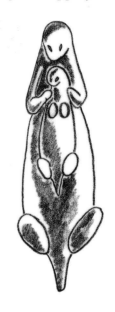

▽ *Fig 14*
The Esquimaux and Inuit peoples, though hunters of the sea otter, respected its ways. Carved ivory or soft stone amulets were thought to bring good fortune.

PLATE 18
The magnificent osprey in full flight. The sweep of the wings pivots to the shoulder joint (see text); similarly the tail fans out from the middle of the rump. Always work from the central point outward: first the feather at the middle of the tail and then, progressively, one side followed by the other. In this way the overall motif will build up evenly, avoiding an unnatural 'pull' on the background fabric.
26 x 36.25cm (10¼ x 14¼in)

Where the sea recedes into a land-locked estuary in Plate 18, its meeting with the shoreline is suggested by a simple abutting of horizontal straight stitches which form the bulk of the landscape. Further into the distance, elements are softened by interspersing upright stitches to create trees and shrubs, the hills stark against the skyline. In the immediate foreground the estuary opens out, its entry into the wider waters of the sea hinted at rather than fully described by the meandering edges of the channel and its smooth baseline. A final touch of continuity is effected by scattered droplets which fly from the fins and tail of the hapless trout. Shaded similarly to the water beneath, they lead the eye back to the sea.

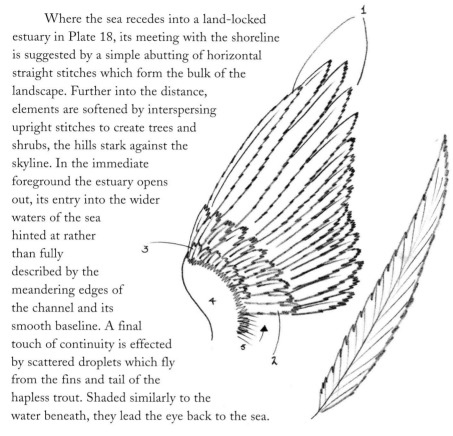

⊲ *Fig 15*
Treat each long primary feather in the same way as a leaf, working directional opus plumarium *down either side of the central quill (right). After shadow lining (if on a pale background) work the primary feathers first (1), followed by the secondary (2) and smaller feathers (3). As many strata as necessary of radial* opus plumarium *radiate outward from the shoulder axis (4). Finally, soften the last stratum, which will abut the inner row of feathers, by subduing the overlap or void (5).*

⊲ *PLATE 19 (Detail of Plate 18)*
When working wing feathers, allow the secondary feathers to overlap the primaries, the tertials to overlap the secondaries, and so on. . .
Delicate markings can be added by straight stitched ticking once the groundwork is complete.
Detail shown: 10 x 7cm (4 x 3in)

CHAPTER TWO

EUROPA

Unroll the embroidery of vermilion and purple.
The richest silks of Argos are prostrated
To honour the King's tread at his homecoming,
And cushion every footfall of his triumph.

Aeschylus (translated by Ted Hughes)
The Oresteia

VOICES FROM THE PAST

PLATE 21 ▷

There are many species of anemone which thrive throughout temperate Europe, both wild and cultivated, from the garden favourite Anemone blanda *to the delicate* A. nemorosa *or windflower – so called, according to Greek writer Pliny, because its petals will not open until the wind blows them the breath of the gods.* A. coronaria, *shown here, is named for the crown of contrasting colour which surrounds the black pollen mass at the centre of each bloom. The variety 'de Caen' brings the hot, rocky Mediterranean coast into our gardens.*

9.5 x 10.25cm (3³/₄ x 4¹/₄in)

◁ *PLATE 20*

We are used to seeing traditional ornamental motifs in stylized form, but by returning them to nature we can begin to appreciate why certain subjects became 'style classics' in the first place. The strength of the thrusting acanthus spear creates an obvious decorative support for buttresses and columns, the elegant coils and arabesques of the grapevine, with its pendulous bunches of fruit is a naturally softening device with which to swathe hard mouldings and masonry, and the pleasing symmetry of the olive branch, together with all its symbolic associations, suggest repetitive designs perfect to ornament dados, cornices and pelmets.

'Classical' fashions dominated Western architecture and interiors from the Renaissance of the early sixteenth century onwards. Neo-classicism originated in France and with the rise of Napoleon a deliberate attempt was made to recapture the splendours of ancient Rome. The style soon crossed the English Channel surfacing as a major element in Regency fashion. In 1817 Rudolph Ackermann (1764–1834) published his Selection of Ornaments, *which includes plenty of inspiration for embroiderers (see Fig 17).*

Embroidery shown life-size:
40 x 27.5cm (15³/₄ x 10³/₄in)

From the cold, craggy fjords of the north to the sun-baked fields of the south a rich seam of archaeology, both physical and anecdotal, runs throughout Europe revealing traces of textile art's earliest history. Perhaps more than any other art form embroidery has always tended to be eclectic in its assimilation of design – successful motifs in other media, from stonework to jewellery and manuscripts, have always found their way, duly re-interpreted, into contemporary or slightly later embroideries. Virgil describes an acanthus embroidered on the gown of Helen of Troy; acanthus being the fashionable ornament of Corinthian columns.

Classical motifs survived the fall of the Hellenistic kingdoms as they were assimilated into the Roman Empire's eastern provinces. The friezes of Pompeii show borders of robes richly decorated with classical patterns – designs which themselves began life as architectural details, and Roman mosaics in Sicily show varied ornaments in bands and medallions of geometric and plant motifs – vine-scrolls were a favourite. An embroidered panel of the fourth century bears a striking resemblance to a floor mosaic in West Sussex, England suggesting that multi-purpose pattern-books were circulated throughout the Empire (Fig 16).

As the Romans withdrew from western Europe after AD400 they were replaced by the Germanic kingdoms whose textile art evolved in part from Iron Age influences (fine embroidery survives from sixth century BC tombs near Stuttgart) and new trends from the Byzantine East. In Britain the Anglo-Saxons produced outstanding silk and gold embroideries and intricate tablet-woven braids, and the trade in expensive and exotic textiles boomed under the free-roaming Vikings who travelled the whole of Europe (and beyond) after AD800.

Plate 20 is a tribute to the classical world. The acanthus (*Acanthus spinosus*), grape vine (*Vitis vinifera*) and olive (*Olea europaea*) were all popular motifs throughout the Hellenistic and Roman Empires and continued to appear in textile design into the Middle Ages and beyond. Here, I have treated them relatively naturalistically, suggesting by the gold and black high and lowlights the glow of a warm Mediterranean sunset.

The acanthus thrives today in many gardens, its showy purple and pink flowers tempting large, strong insects such as bumble bees into their tight, tunnel-like throats to reach the nectar at the base of each bloom. The bees emerge dusted with pollen which they transfer to neighbouring plants. It is easy to see why the acanthus, and especially its broad, leathery leaves, became an architectural cliché (Fig 18). Tradition holds that it was first used by the Greek architect Callimachus when he designed the great temple at Corinth (see *The Embroiderer's Countryside*)

but it soon became a design classic throughout the ancient world, with swags and garlands used to decorate furniture, statuary and clothing. Both flowers and leaves are complicated structures, but, taken apart (Fig 19), can be approached in embroidery stage by stage. It is important to analyze intricate motifs before you begin your work as only by doing so can you begin to understand the form of the subject. Though less convoluted, the grape vine should be treated similarly.

The elegant arabesques of the vine-scroll form another motif which spans the millennia. I have intentionally portrayed the leaves from the two perspectives in which they are traditionally shown – full-faced and in semi-profile, 'cupping' to receive the riches of Bacchus, God of wine. This latter arrangement entails the use of opposite angle embroidery but as the directional sweep of each side of the leaf is, superficially at least, in the same direction, the stitch flow is, in fact, also at the same angle. Again, a careful analysis of each leaf is necessary to achieve the correct effect. Grapes have been cultivated to produce wine since the earliest recorded history, their colour and size dictating the characteristics of the wine they yield. I have chosen a small Corinthian variety (to companion the acanthus!) which traditionally also produces currants. In places not fully ripe, the colour of the fruit ranges from deep purple to golden green, each grape worked in a single stratum of very slightly angled radial *opus plumarium* (the growing point of each is its attachment to the stem). A two-ply, twisted thread of black and metallic gold is surface couched around each grape (terminating before it reaches the apex) to suggest both a shadow line and the glint of the lowering sunset.

The third subject of this study is the olive branch. In ancient Greece the olive was sacred to the Goddess Pallas Athene, and she presented the newly dedicated city of Athens with an olive bow, symbol of peace and fertility. Grecian brides wore or carried sprigs of olive (in the same way the orange blossom became a later tradition) and as a motif it bore similar associations. A crown of olive leaves was the highest distinction which could be bestowed upon a Greek citizen in recognition of service to his country – and it was the 'gold medal' of the ancient Olympics. The fruit of the olive tree, from which olive oil is expressed, has been a valuable export of the Mediterranean for centuries and its wood has a strong grain suitable for turnery. The long, tapering,

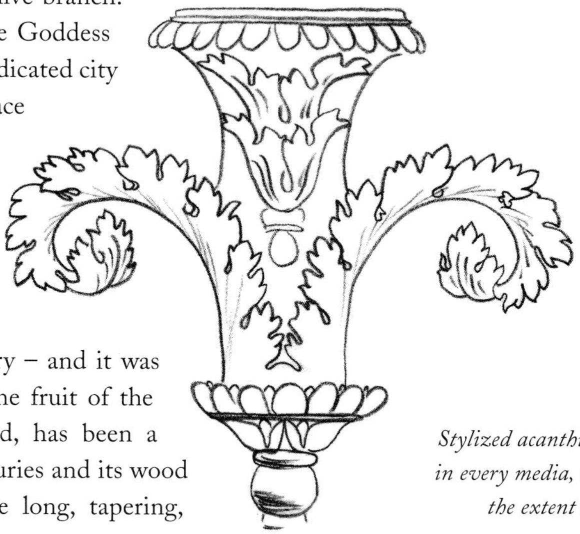

◁ Fig 16
'Autumn', a fourth century embroidery design originating in Egypt showing Roman imperial design at its best – worked closely in split and stem stitch. A companion piece 'Winter' also survives.

△ Fig 17
'Part the Third' of Rudolph Ackermann's early nineteenth century pattern book illustrates how textiles were an integral part of the craze for neo-classicism. Chubby cherubs swathed (or not!) in richly textured and embroidered hangings are features of many major set pieces.

◁ Fig 18
Stylized acanthus has run riot through design in every media, becoming more exaggerated in the extent and habit of its growth.

elliptical leaves are simply worked in directional *opus plumarium*, and the full-bodied, blue-black fruits in bold single strata of radial work overlaid with a highlight of white straight stitching.

This chapter's opening quote from the ancient writer Aeschylus emphasizes the important symbolism of colour. Agamemnon is returning to Argos after the defeat of Troy, the richest textiles of the royal household laid before him as he enters the city. Purple dye was a costly luxury (obtained in tiny amounts from shellfish): to tread upon it an outstanding honour. For centuries all dyes were 'natural', obtained more usually from plants and lichens, altered and enhanced by ores and other additions, various civilizations developing their own favourite methods. Thus, motifs gleaned from the natural world and materials such as linen flax and dyestuffs derived from plants came together to form the basis of embroidery's almost incestuous relationship with nature. Apart from simplistic geometric designs most surviving evidence of primitive embroidery is based upon floral or foliate designs.

Plates 21 and 22 show modern and ancient interpretations of simple, open-faced flowers. The pretty, red anemone (*Anemone coronaria*) is one of the first Mediterranean flowers to appear in the spring. Modern chemical dyes allow easy access to silks in deep, vibrant colours and whilst the technique of radial *opus*

PLATE 22 ▷

Saxon and Anglo-Viking graves have revealed most of our surviving physical evidence of early Northern European textiles. The central panel of this reconstruction is described in the text; with it are materials and tools authentic to the post-Roman period from the fifth to the eighth century. Silks (right) are hand spun, and although they lack the sophistication of the smooth floss silks of the turn of the ninth century (see Plate 6, page 11) they still possess a vibrant glow made richer by the addition of surface couched gold and silver thread (top left). The faceted, boss-headed pin (centre left) is the type which might well have been used to transfer designs onto fabric (pricking and 'pouncing' with powdered dye), and seed pearls (bottom left) were a popular, though costly, addition. The medallion is suspended on a woollen tablet-woven braid.

Height of medallion: 7.5cm (3in)

plumarium enhances the sweep of shades which can be effected with a single colour, we can achieve subtle variations by deepening the tone of the petals away from the imagined light source – in this case from the top right-hand quadrant. Embroiderers from before the turn of the last millennium, however, had fewer options. Plate 22 shows a embroidered motif composed of various elements of Scandinavian and Saxon designs and worked on pure, dense evenweave linen in hand-spun silk coloured by plant dyes of the period. Two shades of pink have been achieved by using madder (*Rubia tinctorum*) – its very name implying its ancient use! – dyed in a copper, whilst weld, tansy and dyer's greenweed achieve yellows, or greens with the addition of iron. Simple radial and directional *opus plumarium* have been used together with a little needleweaving in yellow and green together. This type of motif might well have formed decoration on the costume of a middle status, fairly well-to-do land-owner or trader. Silver and gold thread or the addition of seed pearls (as here) would indicate greater prosperity.

THE GOOD EARTH

Whilst the trade in textiles flourished in Europe throughout the Middle Ages – as did commerce in luxuries such as fine pottery, jewellery, spices and other exotic commodities – the undisputed seat of wealth and power still lay in the land. As cities grew and prospered on trade, perhaps only to decline again when they fell victim to siege, war or a simple downturn in prosperity, the boundaries of great country estates, farms and field systems often remained unchanged for centuries – indeed many still exist.

Though the removal of hedgerows and the erosion of ditches and earthworks has made the countryside's early character hard to read in some places, in others, particularly in remote rural areas, the crazy patchwork of strips and fields can be found even now. Between the high hedges and deep ditches of tiny winding country lanes, the tapestry of the English countryside is still apparent, the broad arable and grazing meadows of lowland Scotland have changed little in generations and anyone who has motored through the meandering, tree-lined roads of provincial France will have sensed the timeless, rustic qualities of unspoiled areas of continental Europe.

In most European countries animal-drawn farming methods have given way to the tractor. The idealized picture-postcard image of horse and plough followed by flocks of whirling seagulls is now hard to find, but in autumn the quiet chugging of a small, ageing tractor can be just as evocative of the countryside's changeless aspects. In Plate 23 just such a scene has been captured with the use of a variety of straight stitching techniques. The tractor and its driver have been treated impressionistically – there is little to be gained aesthetically by dwelling upon the engineering of the machine: the solid four-square qualities of the chassis, convoluted working parts of the plough, squashy buoyancy of the large wheels and jaunty seat of the ploughman are all suggested by rough shadow lining and etching (see Appendix A, pages 124 and 129), greys and primary colours dashed in around them.

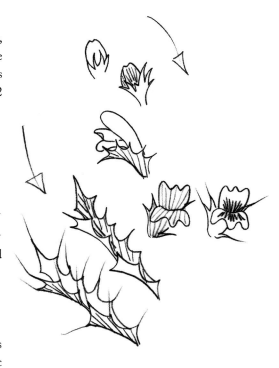

△ *Fig 19*
By mentally divorcing each element of the complicated 'real' acanthus plant we can put it back together with an understanding of how the whole plant 'works'. The stitching on each section should fall back to its own core, sweeping in turn down the length of the frond. Simple buds (top) fall back to their protective prickly sepals, the sepals and open flowers (centre) to their respective growing points. Inner petals are enhanced by shooting stitches (centre right) and leaves are worked in directional opus plumarium *toward their central veins, with opposite angle stitching used where necessary. Finally each prickle is lengthened and sharpened by the addition, through its apex, of a straight stitch in fine thread (bottom).*

The foreground bush and middle distance tree and hedge are 'dressed' in seed stitched leaves – otherwise all the landscape features are straight stitched.

The successful use of what must surely be embroidery's simplest stitch depends upon knowing where to merge, void and abut, or overlap your fields of colour. The sky is suggested by separate patches of single shades in fine single strands of silk, worked evenly and closely. When we reach the horizon, the distant trees are worked in a thicker gauge of silk, in perpendicular stitching, each 'bank' of trees separated by a distinct void. In the furthest swathe of the undulating landscape, we return to horizontal stitching (now in a single strand of mat twisted cotton), allowing the darker shade close to the skyline to merge into the sunlight of the open field, and voids to form between this and the nearer features. The rising land in the middle ground is again voided on all sides. As we enter the near field, the horizontal stitching gradually sweeps around to become oblique and the neat furrows of the ploughed earth are described by alternating shades of light and dark brown. The stubble of the unploughed portion of the field is worked in short perpendicular stitches continuing at the same angle as the long furrow lines. Where the stubble adjoins the first cut of the plough the short stitches overlay their neighbours – this is continued around the machinery and wheels giving the impression of the upright, scratchy stalks standing proud of the ground. In the immediate foreground the headland by the bush returns to horizontal stitching, surmounted by angled, upright grasses.

The recumbent figure of the 'Sleeping Giant' dominates the skyline of Dalnair in lowland Scotland now as it has for centuries (Plate 24). This delightful scene captures the essence of life on the land: the farmhouse proclaims its dominion over the landscape, first the garden, then the surrounding orchard of trees and the rolling fields down to the boundary river. Beyond, the hills begin to rise to the craggy summit of the 'Giant' whilst in the foreground, framing features encompass the wild flowers and insects of a remembered childhood. This picture was commissioned to encapsulate personal memories of time and place. In designing an embroidery such as this the principles of accumulated perspective, discussed in the previous paragraph, are all important.

▽ *Fig 20*
Like the tractor in Plate 23, the combine harvester (right) and potato cropper have been very loosely sketched. Translated into embroidery, the heavy shadows would be dashed and etched into place before the rest of the colours and contours. These will give a framework around which to build the 'impression' of the rest of the machine. Later, detail can be added in the shape of stubble, etc.

Depth is achieved by drawing the eye through the framing features – as we are looking *down* on the farmhouse the effect is to suggest that these features are situated on high ground immediately before us – and on into the body of the work. The colours in the foreground are echoed by those in the main picture; the pinky-mauve of the thistle flowers is repeated in the lowest strata of clouds and the blue of the butterfly in the glinting river water. Above all, the open, airy aspect of the landscape is repeatedly strengthened by the simple device of leaving 'space' between features: in the foreground this is left completely free of stitching; within the landscape itself by allowing broad stretches of straight stitching to flow uninterrupted across the background fabric.

△ *PLATE 23*

In this design the male and female pheasant are miniaturized in some detail – in contrast to the impressionistic treatment of the tractor and its driver – see Plate 27 and Fig 23. Much of this landscape is worked in plied or twisted silk or cotton, the sheen of the floss silk used on the birds provides a variety of texture which helps to set them apart from the rest of the scene.

14 x 15.25cm (5¼ x 6in)

. . . .

. . . .

Many species of flora, fauna and insects span large and diverse habitats in both island and mainland Europe. As well as migrant birds, many butterflies travel vast distances to favoured breeding sites whilst plants, though some may be adopted as heraldic or other symbols of certain nations, can be even more surprising in their choice of environment and confusing in their localized names (see *Helen M. Stevens' Embroidered Butterflies* and *Embroidered Flowers*). The English bluebell (*Hyacinthoides non-scripta*) thrives in Scotland – shown to the left in Plate 24 – although north of the border it is called the wild hyacinth, the name 'bluebell' reserved for the English harebell (*Campanula rotundifolia*) (Fig 21). Similarly the spear thistle (*Cirsium vulgare*) right, is the originator of Scotland's national emblem, although in its homeland the acanthus thistle (*Onopordum acanthium*) is often called the Scottish thistle! It is, at any rate, easy to see why this plant should have been given its Latin name – its leaves are indeed acanthus-like (Fig 19 and Plate 20).

The goldcrest (*Regulus regulus*) shown in Plate 25, together with the firecrest (see Chapter Six) is Europe's smallest bird at only 9cm (3½in) and has been called the highland humming-bird as it will hover like its namesake before darting into the cover of its favourite shrubs and trees – usually conifers. One of nature's textile artists, it weaves an intricate nest of spiders' web, lichen and moss in which it will lay an enormous brood of up to thirteen eggs twice a year. Potentially, one pair of goldcrests can be responsible for a million tons of progeny in eleven years! No wonder this appealing little bird can be found from northern Scandinavia to the Mediterranean. A tiny bird can prove a challenging exercise in embroidery as all the principles of full-sized *opus plumarium* come together in a realistically sized, though very small, subject.

Unlike miniaturization (see Appendix A, page 129) used on the pheasants in Plate 23, in Plate 25 the life-like sweep of the plumage, the differentiation between large feathers, the detail of the face markings, must all be worked without 'shorthand' abbreviations. If working on a pale background, shadow line carefully, using fragmented stitches where the fluffy feathers would break through a smooth outline. Soften hard lines and subdue voiding with a single fine strand of silk, working outwards to 'feather' the effect and pay particular attention to details such as the beak and eye highlight. In a study such as this, where the subject appears to be snuggled down into its surrounding of yew foliage, work the needles first so that the radial *opus plumarium* of the body can be flooded (with the appropriate voiding) between them, keeping the angles of the stitching accurate. Remember that detail on the twigs is important too. Each yew needle is worked in a chevron stitch, previously shadow lined and angled back toward the core of the motif. Berries nestle in the foliage bringing an extra touch of vibrant colour.

. . . .

◁ *PLATE 25*
The tiny goldcrest is so tolerant of human
companionship that it will continue its hunt
for insects through raspberry and loganberry
canes whilst they are being pruned! Unlike
its rivals, its apparent indifference to being
watched makes it a superb subject for quick
sketching. Even if you are not confident of
capturing fine details in situ *make a rough*
drawing whenever your subject permits
(see Fig 22). Geometric shapes and
directional notations help to bring the lifelike
'jizz' back to mind when you add the other
features later – perhaps with reference to a
good field guide.
10.75 x 8.25cm (4¹⁄₄ x 3¹⁄₄in)

HOME AND AWAY

Old World countryside which has not disappeared beneath the bricks, concrete and asphalt of cities and motorways or survived as agricultural land has, in many places, been moulded by man to accommodate his leisure activities. Whilst there is, arguably, a dubious moral code in maintaining wild habitats for the purposes of hunting its inhabitants, it is certainly true that managed land, whether wooded, open or sculptured specifically to its new role, makes up a valuable percentage of modern Europe's unspoiled acreage. Country parks, set aside for walking and wildlife watching, flooded gravel pits and other excavations now the setting for water sports, riverside trout farms for anglers, bridleways and cross country courses, even private airstrips for light aircraft and gliders, all provide relatively undisturbed habitats for native or visiting animals and birds. A well maintained golf course, whether the windblown links of coastal areas or the landscaped, wooded and bunkered havens of the English home counties can provide a wealth of design opportunities.

The advantage of the 'tame' countryside can be its ease of accessibility. Mountain climbing in the Alps or hiking through the fells of Scotland is not within the physical reach of everyone, but even those with limited mobility may now gain access to safari parks, wildfowl reserves and sporting facilities. With a sketch-book and a pack of crayons in your pocket, and a little patience, you can

PLATE 26 ▷

Like Plate 23, this picture is a composite design, worked for a special occasion – in this case as a presentation gift to a long-serving golf-club committee member. The beautifully maintained golf course, a haven for many wild flowers, animals and birds, is a marvellous subject but there needs to be 'action' in the middle ground to focus the attention before the eye is led away into the distance. Badgers (Meles meles), *although mainly nocturnal, often begin their foraging whilst it is still light in the summer and they eat a wide variety of food, from earthworms to small mammals, ground-nesting birds, reptiles, amphibians, fish and insects. The attention of the adult has been engaged by the whirring flight of the dragonflies. Though generally wary, if their confidence is not abused they will tolerate human company – especially if food is involved – and have been known to loiter under street lamps to snap up cockchafer beetles in flight, attracted to the light.*

Embroidery shown life-size:
26.5 x 21.5cm (10½ x 8½in)

bring the natural world back to your drawing board and ultimately your embroidery frame.

An important element of enjoying the design process is letting go of your fear! Whilst it is a gift, of course, to be able to sketch spontaneously from life, it is one which few of us can claim to enjoy naturally – but there are a wealth of good textbooks and inspirational magazines and photographs to give us the fine details of a subject's anatomy. More important is the overall composition of a rough sketch which can later be translated into a detailed design. Plate 26 is a composite pattern suggested by the elements which could be observed (with luck!) on a certain golf course. Needless to say, it is unlikely that any observer would be fortunate enough to witness the scene exactly as shown – I was told there were badgers resident in the area – but the rest of the component parts, the flowers, foliage, dragonflies, geese in flight and distant scenery were all there to be enjoyed.

Split your design into at least three planes – foreground or framing features, middle ground (this is usually where the 'action' is taking place) and distance. As you enjoy your surroundings, don't be embarrassed to take out your sketch-book and make rough 'notes' (see Fig 22). You may be impressed by a repetitive geometric shape which appeals to your design sense – jot it down. There may be something about the colour tones of a scene which captures the moment – make a note. When you take your sketch-pad back home is the time to worry about fine details – for now, just feel the atmosphere.

Fig 22 ▷
The composition of Plate 26 is built on a framework of triangles. The stocky badgers in the middle ground are framed by a foreground of more acute angles and broader backdrop features. I was rather taken with this 'Picasso-esque' design and almost loathed to refine it into a sensible pattern! Don't be afraid to be bold with your initial sketches – nobody need ever see them but you!

Plate 26 shows a sun-drenched early summer morning. Predominant colours are yellow and gold complemented by the blue of the water and sky. Greens are suffused with yellow, or silvery-blue, to tone with the other features, and the angular qualities of the badgers echo other elements of the overall scene. All the landscape techniques used here have been discussed earlier in this chapter and once again, as in Plate 23, miniaturization has been employed in the flying birds. These are shown in detail in Plate 27.

The process of miniaturization is certainly helped by a familiarity with your subject. My studio is deep in the Suffolk countryside, close to flooded gravel pits, now the home to hundreds of Canada geese (*Branta canadensis*) whose trumpet-like hooting and honking can suddenly reach a crescendo as they take wing from nearby grassland and head for the water. They fly in triangular 'skein' formation, the lead bird describing a ramrod-straight line towards its target, the rest of the squadron an arrow behind him. Their tameness makes them an excellent subject for study at close hand, their regular aerobatic performances allowing distance work, too. The all-important key to miniaturization is to recognize and extrapolate the essential characteristics of your subject. The basic rules of directional stitching still apply, but each stitch must fulfil the purpose of several dozen full-sized stitches (see Fig 23).

Canada geese were introduced into Europe from North America as early as the 1600s as decorative birds for parkland lakes. Their toleration of human company probably, conversely, saved them from becoming popular game birds, as this, coupled with their low, slow flight, was in later centuries considered to make them too poor a 'sporting target' for shooting and they are now established as successful breeding birds in Britain and Sweden, moving further south for the winter.

Man's interference with the natural order of the countryside has not always been so benevolent though. Butterfly collecting has been a popular pastime for

◁ PLATE 27 (Detail of Plate 26)
To miniaturize a subject successfully all the basic rules of establishing a light source and directional stitching still apply (Fig 23). Here, the Canada geese are shown in a variety of poses, wings outstretched, upright and in their downward sweep to give an illusion of movement to the flight. In all cases, the underside of each motif has been carefully shadow lined, individual primary feathers suggested, and markings emphasized. It is particularly important to finish off your work neatly in miniature embroidery, as any stray 'tails' at the back will show through the fabric with greater emphasis due to the delicacy of the surface work. You may need to use three or four shades on each small motif. Each thread must be worked into the back of the stitching separately. Never 'jump' from one subject to the next, even on a black background, as the texture of the thread may disturb the smooth surface of the intervening fabric.
Detail shown: 8.25 x 3cm (3¼ x 1¼in)

centuries, though now, thankfully, increasingly conservation conscious times have made it less acceptable. More of a threat to the survival of rare species is the destruction of habitat. The beautiful swallowtail butterfly, once common in Britain, now maintains a perilous foothold in only a very few locations – one of which, the Norfolk Broads, is managed as a holiday location for sailing and other water sports. The so-called scarce swallowtail (*Iphiclides podalirius*) is a rather more populous butterfly in continental Europe where it occurs from north of the Alps and into the Baltic to the southern Mediterranean. It is shown in Plate 28 with mock orange blossom (*Philadelphus*).

Swallowtail butterflies (*Papilionidae*) have attracted a great deal of attention from collectors and many species are now protected in various countries (see also

◁ *Fig 23*
Whilst a quick sketch (below) can be lacking in detail, to achieve a successful miniature it is necessary to include all the basic elements of a subject when preparing a design for transfer (centre). Individual primary feathers are particularly important to give the bird reality and these should be shadow lined as on a full-size study. Each feather might then need only six to eight stitches to convey it, but these must follow the usual rules of directional flow (top).

· · · · · · · · ·

Plate 62 in Chapter Six). The thrill of the chase has always motivated butterfly hunters: rare swallowtails were once traded for vast sums of money and, sadly, in some cases still are. Attempts to rear them on butterfly farms have met with varied degrees of success, as has re-introduction, in places, into their natural habitat. Glasshouse breeding environments provide, nevertheless, a marvellous opportunity for watching and interpreting these fabulous insects at close range. Most hand-reared butterflies have no fear of humans and will alight on coloured clothing, clambering over proffered fingers onto exotic flowers at the closest of quarters. Again, never leave home without your sketch-book! The iridescent sheen of a butterfly's wing is a subject which translates exquisitely into embroidery. Smooth radial *opus plumarium* flooded around Dalmatian spotting or bars and strata in contrasting colours, especially if worked in pure, untwisted silk, captures the effect perfectly – a subject I have explored in detail in *Helen M. Stevens' Embroidered Butterflies*.

Plate 28 couples the scare swallowtail with a simple design companion in the mock orange. The vibrancy and complex wing shape of the butterfly is enhanced by the calming effect of the cool white blossom and the simple, elliptical leaves. The petals and foliage, worked in single strata of radial and directional *opus plumarium* respectively, are borne on stems of narrow, reflexing stem stitch, colours confined to a bare minimum. The only touch of added sparkle is in the butterfly's antennae, worked in a fine strand of gold metallic thread. There are times when it is unnecessary to enhance nature's inherent glamour, even if it occasionally needs a little practical assistance to survive.

CHAPTER THREE

THE SANDS OF TIME

. . . the moon's still pale light picked out
vast sweeping stretches of distance.
Count the stars, as delicate as drops of dew on a spider's web
. . . like a net, so beautiful, so very silent. ￮

Colleen McCullough
The Thorn Birds

DUNE

Deserts are landscapes of sharp and sudden contrast. Baking hot during the day, gauzy mirages quivering above the motionless silk of the sands; ice cold at night, the stars pinpricks of shattered shisha in the black samite of the sky. In spring, brief, violent rains bring the dunes to life in a vibrant riot of flowers, before the aching extremes of temperature settle back, reducing the scene to a tracery of self-coloured damask patterns: dry branches against the sky, fallen trees prone in the brittle, whispering grasses, the debris of flash floods and lightning strike fires littering the ground.

Even in these apparently inhospitable habitats, some flora and fauna thrive, adapting their lifestyles to the rigour of their environments, developing defences against the hardships of heat and minimalism. As for human habitation, a nomadic lifestyle is best suited to these harsh conditions. Even in the vastness of the Sahara desert nomadic peoples survive, their traditions and culture intact after centuries of life in the shifting sands. In the mountains of the Sahara there is evidence of human occupation dating back to the third millennium BC. These lost tribes left evidence of their heritage in wall paintings of wild and domestic animals, self portraits of hunting parties and even a tantalising glimpse of ceremonial costume – figures can be seen dancing in extravagant head-dresses and masks.

It has been suggested that these ancient peoples were the ancestors of the Tuaregs who still live in the south central mountains of the Sahara, principally in southern Algeria. Tuareg men continue to wear traditionally decorated robes and distinctive head-dresses. These often take the shape of a tubular mask with a horizontal front slit to allow for air and vision, surmounted by a flat, fabric cap with vertical brims, frequently embroidered in self-coloured thread. These 'people of the veil' (Fig 25) work exquisite geometric patterns in chain, eyelet, Romanian, satin and straight stitch. Saddle bags and harnesses are also embroidered, a tradition which is widespread throughout north Africa.

Throughout the deserts of the world indigenous peoples have protected themselves from the rigours of the climate by using natural textiles for protection or ceremonial incantation. The native North American tribes (see Chapter Four) developed complex patterns to reflect their harsh environment. Even in Australia, where the aboriginal inhabitants (until their lifestyle was disrupted by settlers) disdained the use of clothing as such, created costume with an intertwining and weaving of grasses and flowers to enhance their body paint.

Plate 29 reflects the harsh environment of the central Australian desert, together with elements of the slightly less austere regime which swings into action after long-awaited rainfall. Like the desert itself, it is a study in contrasts. The red sands, after a rare rainfall, are interspersed with briefly flowering plants which nevertheless thrive in the otherwise arid conditions. The respite is still to reach the branches of the scrubby trees − leaves are not yet in evidence − and in places the long drought has beaten some bushes into submission: they are fallen.

Australia's unique fauna are a joy to explore − subjects which are strangely familiar and yet alien to other continents. The honey possum (*Tarsipes spencerae*) is the smallest marsupial of Australia's 120 species, a tiny mouse-like animal that feeds on the nectar and pollen of flowers, shown in Plate 29 with the large, powder-puff bloom of *Banksia serrata*, one of the few banksia to originate from the east of the continent. The possum's prehensile tail acts as a fifth limb to support it amid the fluffy head of the flower, its long whippy tongue able to penetrate the florets to seek out the nectar at the base of each. Occasionally small insects are also taken, their tough wings discarded, the tender bodies an additional source of rare and valuable protein. Scrambling up the succulent stem of the banksia is the 'club-pod' (*Gompholobium polymorphum*), a member of the huge, international, pea family.

Whilst all these species are unknown in the 'Old World', and may be equally unexpected as embroidery subjects, they can be described in techniques which are as familiar as the animals and plants of which they might remind us. The possum (like any small rodent, for instance see Plate 7, page 12) should be worked in smoothly advancing strata of radial *opus plumarium*, voiding softened by an over stitching of fine silk. The head of the banksia we might approach similarly to the bloom of a familiar multi-floret wildflower (Fig 27), its corolla of leaves in directional *opus plumarium*, and the coiling tendrils of the club-pod are worked in reflexing stem stitch and surface couching. Though the landscape itself seems other-worldly, this effect is achieved largely by the choice of the black background. The trees are worked in straight and stem stitch, but left 'undressed' of leaves, while finer gauges of thread are chosen for the more distant subjects, to enhance the perspective. Seed and straight stitching conveys an impressionistic treatment of the wildflowers.

Sir Joseph Banks (1743−1820), after whom the banksia is named, was responsible for the identification and classification of many wildflowers,

◁ *Fig 25*
The Tuareg are a handsome, predominantly fair-skinned people who are among the most settled of the nomadic Berbers of North Africa. 'The Blue Men of the Sahara', their skin is often stained by the indigo dye of their veils and robes, embroidered in self-coloured threads. A portrait such as this would make a successful miniature in the style of Plate 52 (page 88) − the unchanging fashions of the desert could partner him with the medieval lady in Fig 45 (page 89) to produce an attractive pair.

◁ *Fig 26*
Bushtail possums were originally forest dwellers but have followed man into towns and cities for easy pickings and shelter. Like the honey possum in Plate 29, it is a delightful subject.

Fig 27 ▷
The large fluffy head of the banksia (Plate 29) should be approached similarly to any multi-floret subject – only on a grander scale. Here, the musk thistle (Carduus nutans)*, burdock* (Arctium lappa) *and star thistle* (Centaurea calcitrapa) *would each be worked on the same basic principles. The sepals, whether fleshy (left), wispy (centre) or leaf-like (right), should be completed first, the fine down of the flower head built up in ranks, becoming increasingly delicate toward the outer edges.*

△ *Fig 28*
Persia (now Iran) boasts an ancient tradition of embroidery. This form of flower-and-figure motif dates from the sixth or seventh century, designed to be worked in chain stitch. Colour was important – again indigo was a favourite dye (it is one of the most ancient dyestuffs known to man, used since at least 2500BC in the Old Kingdom of Ancient Egypt) – traces of blue, red and green still survive on the original of this piece.

and their introduction from their countries of origin to Europe. Banks, who had previously sailed with Captain Cook on his first voyage to the Pacific, brought the first Persian roses (*Rosa persica*) into England around 1790 after expeditions to the Middle East discovered this lovely plant some thirty years earlier (Plate 30). The Persian rose has been identified with the biblical 'Rose of Sharon' (actually a European hypericum), the confusion being understandable, as the flowers bear a considerable similarity, and the former, unlike its namesake, bears the typical thorns of a rose. The rose motif is stylized in Persian weaving techniques as the 'gol' (see *The Myth and Magic of Embroidery*), an angular adaptation which by the eighteenth century was widely accepted as an embroidery pattern – earlier floral embroidery retained a slightly more naturalistic approach (Fig 28). Plate 30 interprets the Persian rose in a simple, realistic guise.

The shadow line on the yellow flowers has been emphasized to suggest the fierce, bright sunlight of the desert and its consequently deeper shade. Three strata of radial *opus plumarium* describe each petal, orange-red at the centre, paling to apricot and bright yellow, the pollen mass overlaid in straight and seed stitches. A simple 'open-faced' flower such as this is a perfect example of the successful use of radial work – each petal bears a relationship to its neighbour, uniting to create a 'whole' bloom, rather than a collection of disjointed petals. The sequence of stitching is explained in Fig 29. Short, straight thorns are worked in chevron stitch (Appendix A, page 127) in a broadly alternating pattern along the stems, and extending onto the buds, protecting their succulent interior from moisture-seeking birds and animals.

Animals which survive in harsh desert environments have evolved various ways of dealing with heat and cold. The fennec fox (*Vulpes zerda*) has a dense, soft coat which insulates it from extremes of temperature, and huge triangular ears alert to the tiniest scamper in the sands (Plate 31). Favourite prey include gerbils and jerboas (Saharan and Middle Eastern equivalents of the honey possum) whose vegetarian diets include such delicacies as the occasional, hotly disputed, rosebud.

Working white filling stitches on a black background is the ultimate challenge to the effectiveness and versatility of *opus plumarium*. It also requires the use of other subtle techniques, such as voiding, subdued voiding and feathering. The core or 'growing point' on most animals is the nose – this is the fulcrum back towards which all the stitches will flow. Once this is established, concentric strata of radial work are built up gradually, allowing voids to form where one plane crosses another – for instance, where the muzzle and chin jut forward, the cheek lies across the body, the body crosses the leg and vice versa. These voids should be softened by an overstitching of fine feathering (straight stitches extending beyond the last strata of *opus plumarium*), the feathering continuing uninterrupted where the main corpus of the stitching is worked against the background fabric. Thus, the softening of the voids appears to be a natural extension of the fluffy outer coat (see also the sea otters in Plate 17, page 30).

The stark beauty of the desert sands can be emphasized in a variety of ways. Smooth, horizontal straight stitching is the simplest and most effective method of suggesting monotonous, undulating dunes, but remember that sands vary in their colour and texture as widely as more fertile soils. The sands of the Sinai Peninsula may be golden brown (Plate 31), whereas the unforgiving plains of the Australian outback are brick red, and scattered with scrubby, low-lying, greenish vegetation (Plate 29). Except at the heart of vast, uninterrupted desert such as the Sahara, sand textures are rarely uniform: pebbles and stones break the monotony and these can be suggested by dramatic additions such as the tiny uncut gemstones, amethyst, aquamarine and blue topaz in Plate 31. The icy, surreal beauty of the desert at night can be mirrored by shattered fragments of shisha glass (Plate 29), frost-fractured stones suggested by a criss-crossing of anchoring stitches in clear cellophane blending filament.

ON REFLECTION

Indian mirror work, correctly called *shishadur*, is most famously produced in Balchistan (now in Pakistan), and is traditionally created by attaching small round pieces of silvered glass to the background fabric by a retaining web of stitches around the circumference of the circle. Originally, the concept was to frighten away evil spirits, who, seeing myriad reflections of themselves in the mirrors, would flee in terror. Modern shisha embroidery employs tiny glass fragments, but in older pieces the mirrors were often more than 3cm (1¼in) across. In Plate 29, I have used angular mirrors (about 2.5cm/1in diameter) broken into irregular shapes. These have been attached to the ground fabric in an adaptation of traditional shisha stitch (see Fig 30). Be *extremely* careful when breaking the glass – shisha mirror is not 'toughened' and can fracture into minute, dangerous slivers. Always shatter the glass

△ *Fig 29*
The Persian Rose.
Top: Identify the shape of each petal, noting where parts of each are hidden behind their neighbours.
Second: The direction of the radial opus plumarium *is established, unaffected by the overlap of petals.*
Third: Three strata of radial work describe the colours and markings on each petal.
Bottom: Stamens are overlaid in straight stitch and tipped with seed stitches to complete the pollen mass.

. . . .

inside a closed bag, then tip the shards into an open dish so that you can pick them out carefully. Dispose of the remnants safely.

Mirrors produce a hard effect – an actual image – but for softer effects, we can use the idea of reflection to create a sense of tranquillity, meditation and rest. At Agra, close to Delhi in central Northern India, stands one of the world's most exquisite tributes to love and loss – the Taj Mahal (Plate 32). Built by Shah Jehan in the sixteenth century, it is the tomb of his wife, Mumtaz Mahal (her name means the 'Crown of the Palace') who died whilst accompanying her husband on one of his military campaigns. Bringing together the finest craftsmen from all over the world, the Taj was raised as her monument, a symmetrical wonder of marble and inlaid mosaic. Symmetry in itself has a calming effect: in this study I have used both the symmetry of the building as it stands, and as it is reflected in the water of the lake.

As with most man-made structures, the Taj is best worked in perpendicular stitching. Shadows are etched into place in long straight stitches, emphasized where necessary by areas of dashing (see Appendix A, page 129), the main body of the building infilled around them. The domes are worked in needleweaving, straight stitches in an upright alignment subsequently woven through by a finer, darker thread, to suggest the blocks of marble which dominate the roofs. Each element of the building – domes, minarets, windows, columns, alcoves – must be reflected in the waters below. A harsh, inverted 'photograph' of the original can be avoided by changing the alignment of the stitching – in the watery element the horizontal perspective is used. The faint, rippling effect of the waters is emphasized by the fracturing of hard lines into 'steps' of design and colours are softened by an undercurrent of blue which suffuses the whole reflection. See also the detail of this picture in Plate 9, page 14.

Trade in Indian textiles extended across the sub-continent. Whilst many areas produced their own readily recognisable styles, techniques were in places interchangeable, and tributaries of the Silk Route (see Fig 48, page 92) which spanned the whole of India, Asia and the Middle East meant that threads, fabrics and dyes were a ready source of commerce. However, whilst the items embroidered might be similar – wall hangings, rugs, accessories and clothing – the people of each region produced (and still do) motifs and designs remarkably dissimilar in concept. Bengal, to the east, has long been the home of *tussur* silk, produced by the wild silkworm *Antheraea paphia*, the characteristic yellow silk used for both ground fabric and embroidery thread. Today, Bengal is divided between Bangladesh and India and is one of the world's most densely populated regions. Survival is a hard business and no scraps of textile, however old, are allowed to go to waste. Rag embroideries, or *kanthas*, are pieced together from old saris and other fragments, the resulting jigsaw of fabric richly decorated with lines of running stitch and back stitch. Kantha embroidery is worked and designed by women – the motifs steeped in tradition. Geometric, floral and animal patterns are all popular, the latter marvellously naïve and lively (see Fig 31).

The animals in Fig 31 reflect the beasts which share the Bengalis' world. The tiger is shown prone – perhaps its portrayed demise is thought to invoke protection again man-eaters. Nowadays, in the West, we are more likely to want to preserve this beautiful creature in its natural habitat, anxious to find ways in which man and tiger can both survive. The Bengal tiger (*Panthera tigris tigris*), Plate 33, is a solitary cat whose territory can extend up to 100sq km (39sq miles). Over such a large expanse, terrain may well vary from hot, dry, dusty scrublands, to verdant jungle – water holes in dryer landscapes are valuable assets to a tiger; not just a place to

◁ *PLATE 31*
The enchanting fennec fox is one of the North African desert's most successful small predators. Its diet mainly consists of beetles, termites and other insects – its huge ears acting like radar dishes, swivelling to catch the slightest rustle of movement. To protect their delicate interior from heat and sand, the ears are thickly covered with fine, downy fur, which allows only glimpses of the pink flesh within.
Work the ears in broadening strata of radial opus plumarium. The two innermost strata should be in a different texture to the outer, suggesting the mat surface of the inner ear, gradually giving way to silky fur. This is then overlaid with shooting stitches to subdue the voiding at the base of the ear and soften the strata. Work a fine feathering at the outer edges to emphasize the fluffy outline.
16.5 x 15.25cm (6½ x 6in)

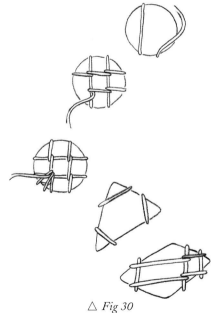

△ *Fig 30*
Traditionally shisha mirrors are round and therefore need substantial anchoring to the base fabric to ensure their stability: first loosely attached, then whipped in place across and around the edge of the glass. Angular fragments are more easily attached, but be careful to use enough anchoring stitches on larger pieces. Whipping at least once is a good idea.

HELEN M.
STEVENS

Kantha designs from Bengal are delightfully naïve and lively. Simple designs such as this could form the basis of an embroidery as a gift for a small child – or even to introduce the youngest members of the family to the joys of stitching for themselves.

◁ *PLATE 32*
The beautiful Taj Mahal is an enduring homage to love. This picture was commissioned to commemorate an Indian marriage, and includes not only this well-known image and other local motifs, but also allusions personal to the couple involved. The orchids (Coelogyne nitida) and peacocks are both symbols of love and of India itself whilst the mango (Mangifera indica) (top left) is a native of the area. Mangoes have been cultivated in India for over four thousand years and currently occupy over two million acres – inevitably it is a motif used in many textile art forms. The egg-shaped fruits are mirrored here by a hot-air balloon – not a traditional element of the scene! On their honeymoon, the couple were fortunate to be able to fly over the Taj and enjoy a rare glimpse of its magnificent architecture from above. In common with much traditional Indian art, I have tried to retain an element of formal, stylized, symmetrical design.
Embroidery shown life-size:
21.5 x 28cm (8½ x 11in)

drink, but also a good spot in which to catch prey unawares. After years of persecution by hunters, in 1972 the World Wide Fund for Nature, together with the Indian government launched 'Project Tiger', establishing more than forty tiger reserves and giving the species the full protection of a trade ban on all tiger products. Despite the continued activities of poachers, the Bengal tiger now has a real chance of survival.

The cat family is (as far as I have been able to observe) the only animal group which, interpreted through the medium of radial embroidery, does not share the almost universal 'nose tip' growing point or core for stitching, as described above. In the case of the cat, whether large or small, the core is on the bridge of the nose, at the point at which the 'stop' begins to rise toward the forehead. This very characteristic nap of the fur is important if we are to capture a lifelike portrait. In Plate 33 the tiger's face is worked in narrow strata of split stitch – by treating the split stitch as though it were *opus plumarium* we can achieve the effect of short smooth fur, gradually lengthening towards the jowl and neck, at which point radial *opus plumarium* takes over. This sequence of stitching may be used on any feline subject – Plate 34 shows Buster, a fine marmalade and white shorthair. Like the tiger his fur pivots through 360 degrees on the bridge of his nose, shorter stitches giving way to longer as the face broadens.

The black background chosen to set off the 'burning bright' tiger has been mounted onto a round backing board (see Appendix B). This surmounts a deep

PLATE 33 ▷

'What immortal hand or eye could frame thy
fearful symmetry?' wrote William Blake in
1794. Certainly the dramatic black and orange
stripes of the Bengal tiger, together with its
silver-white highlights make it a challenging
subject. Fine details, such as the speckles on the
muzzle, chin and nose should be added in
studding (see Appendix A, page 127) after the
main body of the stitching is complete. The
smooth white spot on the back of each ear should
be in Dalmatian dog technique, black opus
plumarium flooded around it. These white
spots are 'eyes' in the back of the tiger's head to
confuse other animals and should be
emphasized. The white highlights in the tiger's
real eyes are all important; by setting them
slightly off-centre, the pupils are given more
importance and the eyes seem to follow the
viewer. Like the fennec fox, the tiger's ears are
all important in its hunting. They are similarly
protected by a dense, fine fur which can be
worked at the same time as the feather-like
softening of the outermost strata.
7.5 x 7.5cm (3 x 3in)

green fabric (mounted onto a backing in the usual way) to suggest the dark recesses of the Indian night jungle. Never be afraid to experiment with presentation, though steer clear of 'fussy' backgrounds or surrounds and mounts unless they are chosen with a particular purpose in mind – see Plates 59 and 70 in Chapters 6 and 7.

However fine a thread may be, it has to be cut across its width to give the required length: this results in a 'blunt' end to the thread. Whiskers, on the other hand, taper to a fine tip, and the magnificent bristling whiskers of the tiger are no exception. Buster's white whiskers, against a pale background, work well enough in a fine (though not hair-like) silk – they need to be substantial to show up against the cream. On black, however, they might be overwhelming – a problem which taxed my imagination whilst working the tiger portrait. My own cat offered the solution. . . whiskers moult and are shed like any other fur. After several months of searching, enough discarded whiskers were found to complete the embroidery – couched down along their length with a gossamer fine white silk thread. Now, any cast-off whiskers are all retained in a special treasury – ready for use on the next cat portrait!

◁ PLATE 34
*'The fat cat on the mat. . . walks in thought
unbowed, proud, where loud roared and fought
his kin', J.R.R. Tolkein reflects that the smallest
feline is kin to the tiger. Buster's marmalade
and white markings, his steady eyes and alert
ears all betray his ancestry, and techniques
similar to the tiger portrait are used here to
capture the spirit of the cat.*
10.25 x 10.25cm (4 x 4in) including frame

CROWN JEWELS

The imperial lily or Crown Imperial (*Fritillaria imperialis*) (Plate 35) is a native of northern India, Persia (now Iran), Afghanistan and the Himalayas. It is one of the oldest known cultivated plants, possibly dating back to the fabled Hanging Gardens of Babylon and the royal courts of the Egyptian Pharaohs. An ancient legend tells that it grew in the Garden of Gethsemane, along with other flowers, all of which bowed their heads as Christ passed by – all except the imperial lily, which was too proud on account of its own magnificent crown. Our Lord rebuked the plant, which hung its then white head in shame, blushed to its current shade of rosy-orange and shed tears of humility. And so it has remained ever since – lift its head and you can still see the tears (actually drops of sticky nectar) hanging within the bells.

As a motif it is certainly regal and the upright 'crown' of leaves bear a striking, stylized resemblance to designs apparently showing the sacred lotus of the Nile. It is possible that as an inspiration for embroidery it could have found its way via Persia to Mesopotamia and into Syria and Egypt. Motifs with a similar pedigree were found on Tutankhamun's tunic (1324–1335BC). As a modern garden flower it is a useful subject for sketching and presents a good opportunity for opposite angle

△ *Fig 32*

The imperial lily is a study in directional stitching. The growing point is at the base of the crowning leaves and the top of each 'bell', so by analyzing the direction of each element of the design we begin to see the inward flow of the stitching. This would be a startling motif worked simply on a black background.

PLATE 35 ▷

The jewel in the crown of many a formal border, the imperial lily is an exotic import into European gardens. Though the roots give off an unpleasant odour, the tall, stately flowers are well worth this slight inconvenience. The long filaments and anthers descend from the large pendant bells, which are surmounted by tufts of leaves, which rather resemble pineapple tops. In my own garden they are planted against a deep, dark backdrop of conifer hedging, and they would work well embroidered on a black ground fabric. Here, however, I have chosen to show them on a pale background, making use of the shadow line which helps to separate the complex interlace of the 'crown'.

9 x 17cm (3½ x 6¾in)

stitching on the flowers and snake stitch on the crowning leaves (Fig 32).

Plants and flowers were important elements in the stylistic design of textiles in ancient Egypt. The life-giving waters of the Nile flowed through the desert, its banks oases of fertility in the otherwise barren sands. Creatures with an ability to survive in these conditions were venerated and became sacred symbols – in particular the scarab beetle. The scarab, a dung-hoarding insect, was thought to embody the ability to bring forth life out of death and decay. A ball of dung, rounded to precision, was hidden in an excavated chamber, the female beetle laid her eggs in the ball, the larva, when hatched eating its way out of its prison. The parallels between this insect's life cycle and the entombment of the Pharaohs are obvious. Along with the ankh (circle-headed cross), this symbol of life and good fortune was a popular motif, and still holds a magic for those with an interest in ancient beliefs. Plate 36 shows a brooch worked in pure silk with plied and pure gold thread.

Between its forelegs the beetle holds a disc, representing the sun, worked in a surface couched spiral of gold metallic thread, the outlines of the various parts of the scarab worked similarly in various gauges. These fields are infilled with straight stitching and the wing cases overlaid in a fine network of honeycomb stitch (see Appendix A, page 127). Around the motif, gold and black plied thread is surface couched in a random, meandering pattern to give an aura of speckled light. Mounted in a simple brooch setting and protected by a sheet of fine, flexible acetate, this is one of my mother's prize possessions!

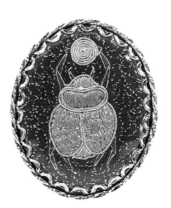

A less exotic but equally attractive motif could be created featuring one of Europe's native beetles, the ladybird (Plate 37). English children have for generations warned ladybirds to 'fly away home'. In France they are more explicit − the Turks have invaded and will spirit away their children into the desert bazaars of the East! Mounted in a slightly more elaborate setting, this brooch is worked similarly to the scarab, in straight filling stitches and surface couched gold thread.

Although working on a tiny scale, the usual principles of presenting your completed embroidery should not be ignored (see Appendix B). Oval or round embroideries should be mounted by working a drawstring around the outside of the piece (previously cut to the appropriate size and shape) which is then drawn up to eliminate rucks and wrinkles in the fabric. Choose a setting which is deep enough to accommodate your mounted work (a delicate miniature will only need a lightweight backing, such as acid-free card) and make sure that the completed piece is aligned correctly − there is nothing more annoying that a 'skewed' miniature. Finally, before protecting with acetate, check that there are no scraps of dust or thread to distract the eye. On a miniature a tiny speck of lint can look like a gargantuan blemish!

◁ Fig 33
The scarab is so rarely shown wings outstretched that it is easy to forget that the dung beetle, like all true members of its family, has delicate and beautiful wings. Occasionally, as here, an ancient design will bear witness to this. See also Fig 44, page 87.

◁ PLATE 36
The various species of dung beetle are dull, dun-coloured insects, well camouflaged in their habitat. The elevation of the scarab to mystical heights, however, allowed artists to make it a more spectacular subject. Turquoise, red and gold are all much used by the ancient Egyptians, and which, against a black background and highlighted by the speckled effect of the meandering plied gold and black silk thread, are seen to stunning effect. A simple, deckle-edged setting is all that is needed to set off this vibrant subject.
4.5cm (1¾in) high, including setting

◁ PLATE 37
The ladybird brooch is worked on a deep yellow, fine cotton ground. An element of reality is retained by alternating the use of a shadow line (to the left) with a gold couched highlight. This single strand of metallic gold is also used to outline the spots − a fine void is left between the black discs and the red wing case, which is infilled with the couching. This idea is reversed in the legs, which are outlined in black and infilled with gold. A slightly more ornate setting is chosen for the brooch itself.
4.5cm (1¾in) high, including setting

CHAPTER FOUR

NEW WORLDS

Thou comest, Autumn, with banners. . .
Brighter than the brightest silks of Samarcand,
And, following thee, in thy ovation splendid,
Thine almoner, the wind, scatters the golden leaves!

Henry Wadsworth Longfellow
Autumn

SPIRIT OF PLACE

PLATE 39 ▷

There are over 500 species of passiflora, mainly from warm temperate and tropical parts of the Americas, with a few species originating in Australia and Asia. Passiflora cincinnata *was first discovered by the appropriately named George Gardner in 1837. Sent to Britain, it did not flower until 1868 – a testament to the tenacious work of the keen collectors and horticulturists of the nineteenth century. Like most 'passion flowers' it supports its growth by means of coiling tendrils, which allow it to clamber up other shrubs and trees, or, when cultivated, walls and masonry.*

8.25 x 9cm (3¼ x 3½in)

◁ *PLATE 38*

There is a tale told among the Plains Indians and many other tribes that when the Great Spirit had completed much of his work on creation he strolled one day through the woodlands of what we now call North America. His new world was beautiful. There were mountains and prairies, rivers and lakes, animals of all kinds and great soaring birds which hovered over the landscape on the wings of the wind. But it was quiet. Apart from the rustling of the autumn leaves no sound broke the silence of his creation. 'Song and chatter and laughter should be a part of this beautiful new Earth' thought the Great Spirit, and looking around for something to inspire his magic, he saw the red and gold leaves flutter to the ground. With a wave of his hand the leaves began to change: instead of falling, they flew high into the sky, wings appeared and beaks opened, melodies floated upward into the air, piping laughter scattered into the treetops and a thousand chirrups and chirps brought the once mute landscape to life.

Embroidery shown life-size:

38 x 26cm (15 x 10¼in)

When European settlers reached the 'new worlds' of the North and South American continents they were astonished by both the similarities and incongruities of the environments. In the north, many species of trees, shrubs and flowers were almost identical to those they had left behind; birds and animals, too, had a familiarity which made immigrants feel at once homesick and at home. Whilst some birds, such as finches, were indeed old friends and a welcome reminder of mainland Europe, others were seized upon for any shared characteristic which made them suitable surrogates: the north American robin, whilst enjoying few specific features in common with its counterpart in Europe (apart from its splendid red breast) soon became the symbol of Christmas from New England to California as surely as the Eurasian robin has become its harbinger in the old country.

Native North American peoples valued nature as a source of inspiration and design, and, in an environment where textile crops were difficult to cultivate, as a reservoir of raw materials. Much embroidery was geometric in concept – a result of the use of inflexible additions such as porcupine quills and feathers. Before the introduction of glass beads by white traders, porcupine quills were one of the major decorative accessories of the indigenous tribes, especially in the plains and woodlands of the north-east, where the American porcupine was common. Trade in textiles, however, was extensive and patterns spread and intermingled between cultures. Flattened quills (traditionally softened by chewing and often brightly dyed) were attached to the ground fabric by a form of couching (see Fig 34) and created curiously modern 'digital' effects reminiscent of today's computer-enhanced designs! 'Hair-pipe' beads made from the centres of conch shells were popular among the Sioux, whilst the Blackfoot were amongst the tribes to perfect the use of feathers in head-dresses and other clothing.

Eastern and southern tribes such as the Iroquois and Seminoles were among the first to integrate mass manufactured ephemera into their designs. 'Wampum' in the shape of beads, braids and fabrics were valuable trading assets for settlers and whilst the production of traditional 'red Indian' embroidery declined during the long centuries of confrontation between native and 'new' Americans, fresh concepts emerged and techniques adapted to suit them. One of the tribes to perfect beadwork was the Navajo – the technique of securing beads to the ground fabric, 'lazy squaw', whereby several beads are threaded between each stitch has entered the language of all embroiderers.

Though often stylized and geometric, foliate and bird designs form a considerable corpus of North American aboriginal work (Fig 35). The traditional folk-tale of the Great Spirit's creation of song birds inspired me to interpret the story and Plate 38 is the result. As the leaves of the beech tree (*Fagus sylvatica*) turn from green to gold, the little birds take flight: the redpoll (*Acanthis flammea*), nuthatch (*Sitta canadensis*) and song sparrow (*Zonotrichia melodia*), red, copper and amber, open wings echoing the flutter of falling leaves. A passing homage is paid to the geometric tradition in the shape of the triangular arrangement of the subject, otherwise all is life and movement.

The redpoll (left) leans forward, beak open, in anticipation of flight, his folded wings close against the body creating a streamlined profile ready to launch into the breeze. Above him, the nuthatch has just taken to the air, wings outstretched to pump the first updraft beneath his feathers, whilst to the right the song sparrow is already in full flight, the slipstream of the wind bearing him away with the beech leaves. These three studies illustrate perfectly why *opus plumarium* is so named. The ability of the sweeping stitches to imitate the birds' feathers creates an effect unparalleled in any other media – the silk *becomes* the plumage of the birds. Like the open wings of the osprey in Plates 18 and 19, the pivot point of the wings, at the shoulder joints, is the key to describing the birds accurately: analyze the flow of the stitches back toward the core of the stitching (in all cases the beak) and, like a river joining an estuary, allow the secondary stream (the wing stitches) to join the main current.

One of the many joys of nature is its imperfection – a single tattered leaf is more evocative of autumn than a hundred perfect specimens, however glorious their colour. Combine the two, add the scratchy texture of beechmast as the seed cases open to reveal the smooth brown nuts within, and the season comes to life. Directional *opus plumarium* falling back to the central veins of the simple, oval leaves has been worked here in one or two strata of stitching, a basic palette of seven colours mixed and blended in the needle to provide continuity. Opposite angle stitching (see Appendix A, page 126) is used where the leaves reflex. Where holes appear, these have been carefully shadow lined to achieve a continuity with the overall lighting pattern and the directional stitching flooded around the voids with particular attention paid to maintaining the angle of the work – this should be uninterrupted by the breaks in colour and texture.

▽ *Fig 34*
Many tribes of native North American peoples use porcupine quills to create complex geometric designs. Couched to the base fabric, an open zigzag creates a broken texture (top), closely abutted, a more uniform effect (centre) and working with two or more differently coloured quills (below) an even more decorative effect.

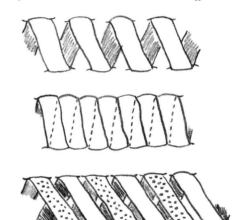

▽ *Fig 35*
Tribal motifs: from the left, a Tlingit eagle design from the far north of North America; centre, Menominee repeating bird-man pattern from north of the Great Lakes; right, floral design from slightly further south, the home of the Ojibwa people.

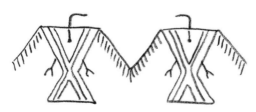

. . . .

In the Old World, beech woods were once an important element of the rural economy. Apart from the use of the timber in furniture manufacture, as it bends beautifully and turns easily (beech chair makers donated the term 'bodgers' to the language as it can be so effectively moulded to enable even apprentices to 'bodge' together a chair), the dense canopy of the beech forest was used to protect animals, fallen nuts and mast were served as food for pigs (and many wild animals) and the thick mat of dead leaves provided a perfect mulch for edible fungi. The four-valved husks of the beech nuts (bottom right in Plate 38) contain (generally) two small, triangular-sectioned nutlets, which detach themselves from the rough, hairy case when ripe. Simple radial and directional *opus plumarium* describe both the husks and the nuts, but the former is overlaid with fine straight stitches crossing the flow of the underlying work to suggest the short, prickly hairs.

An overlay of one technique superimposed upon another is an effective device to describe unusual features. In Plate 39 the halo of filaments forming the corona between the stigma and petals of the passion flower (*Passiflora cincinnata*), a native to many parts of tropical South America, is worked in floating embroidery (see Chapter One). By varying the length of the stitches in accordance with the perspective of the study, a very three-dimensional impression is created. The sweep of the underlying radial *opus plumarium* is uninterrupted by the lightly caught stitches of the floating embroidery which allow the light to penetrate through the foreground work and catch the directional flow beneath.

Like many peoples who survive in extremely hot environments the native cultures of the rain forests have little need for personal adornment in the shape of clothing – textiles are low on their list of priorities – the forest itself provides much of their ceremonial attire. Interaction with Europeans, however, brought the inevitable influx of beads and designs evolved somewhat in common with their Northern counterparts. Similarly symmetrical patterns can also be found in African beadwork and motifs originating in the Middle East. One of the first indigenous inventions 'borrowed' by the Europeans, however, is a textile which had been used on the east coast of Brazil since time immemorial – the hammock. Originally made of woven vegetable fibre yarn, then spun cotton and often decorated, these simple swathes of fabric changed the comfort quota of later sailors beyond all recognition! Early European paintings dating back to the 1500s show similarly spun cotton threads used twined and knotted to decorate head-dresses.

The jungle also provided for most medical needs. In common with the North American 'Indians', native peoples had a broad and effective knowledge of herbalism, which, combined with shamanistic ritual served as healing and preventative treatments. The current trends in natural therapies owe much to the 'medicine men' of the past. St John's wort (Plate 67, page 114) has been hailed as nature's Prozac and the beneficial properties of the various species of evening primrose are well known. Most evening primroses were introduced into Europe in the eighteenth and nineteenth centuries from North and South America – originally garden escapes they are now well established in the wild. The common evening primrose (*Oenothera biennis*) reached England from its native Virginia as

▽ *Fig 36*
Analyze the use of the light source when working details such as tattered foliage. The upper *edge of the hole is the* lower *edge of the surrounding leaf, so this is the contour which should be shadowed.*

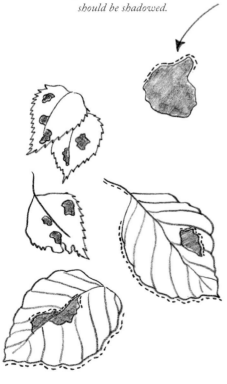

◁ *Fig 37*
Working the Passiflora cincinnata - *from the top clockwise:*
1 The basic outline of the flower, showing the point at which the inner strata of overlay begins. Work the pollen-bearing organs before progressing to the rest of the flower.
2 Establish the flow of the stitching and work the long petals (they are actually sepals, but so petal-like as to be indistinguishable), in a single strata of radial opus plumarium.
3 Work a short inner strata, allowing the stitches to lie slightly more loosely than normal over the longer stitches. (This is a reversal of the usual radial technique – the inner corona of the passion flower appears to stand proud and should therefore be worked separately.)
4 Work two more inner strata following the above guideline.
5 Floating embroidery is overlaid across the whole motif, falling back to the flower centre.

early as 1619. A simple, plate-shaped flower face is an excellent exercise in single strata radial *opus plumarium* (Plate 40) and the symmetrical lanceolate leaves form such an elementary outline that it is tempting to think that they might have both been the inspiration for ethnic embroidery. Some evening primroses have a range from Nova Scotia to Florida, encompassing a multitude of tribes.

Since the early seventeenth century, immigrants from all over western Europe have imported their own styles of embroidery to North America. Among the 'Pilgrim Fathers' who arrived in Plymouth, Massachusetts in 1620 was 'one fustian worker and one silk dyer'. Whilst Puritan custom forbade all 'cutt works, imbroid'd or needle work'd' fripperies, such skills were still valued in many quarters (Fig 38) and the many and varied traditions of both western and later eastern Europe evolved into descendant techniques as diverse as the cultures from which they originated. American samplers, crewel work, needlepoint and in particular quilting deserve their own book to begin to do them justice.

EXPECT THE UNEXPECTED

Emerald, sapphire, amethyst, topaz: a roll-call of humming-birds sounds like a jeweller's inventory as these precious gems of the bird world dart from flower to flower, hovering like bees, then darting forward to sip nectar. There are over three hundred species of humming-bird, mostly confined to tropical America, although some of the most beautiful migrate to the northern continent to breed – reaching as far into temperate and cold areas as south-east Canada and Alaska. Spectacular amongst these is the ruby-throated humming-bird (*Archilochus colubris*), Plate 1 and cover illustration. Wintering in Central America, Mexico and the West Indies, this

△ *Fig 38*
In The Scarlet Letter, *Nathaniel Hawthorne's damning indictment of Puritanism in 1850, Hester Prynne's skill with a needle is respected because of its precision, but incurs disapproval for its 'fancie'. She embroiders the letter 'A' for adultery, which she is forced to wear as evidence of her crime, 'so artistically and with so much fertility and gorgeous luxuriance' that one of her accusers grudgingly has to admit, 'She hath good skill at her needle, that's certain, but did ever a woman, before this brazen hussy, contrive such a way of showing it?'*

. . . .

PLATE 40 ▷

Shown here with herb-Robert (Geranium robertianum), *a native of both Europe and North America, the evening primrose has luminous petals of rich yellow. Day-flowering species are known as 'sundrops', each opening for only one day. Evening-blooming species open for a few hours at dusk (occasionally also at dawn) and attract night-flying insects, especially moths.*

Working a single broad strata of radial opus plumarium *enhances the light-catching qualities of the technique and is particularly effective to describe the delicate, tissue paper texture of several short-blooming flowers – see also the poppies in Plate 10 page 15. Take special care to keep the stitching smooth and, if overlaying other features, such as the stamens, allow these elements to lie quite loosely on top of the underlying work. A large project featuring evening primroses and herb-Robert is included in* Helen M. Stevens' Embroidered Flowers.

8.25 x 10cm (3¼ x 4in)

tiny bird (9cm/3½in long) migrates over 800km (500 miles) – an extraordinary feat for such a small creature. The male's vivid ruby-red throat is softened to a subtle flush of pink in the female (bottom) and, like all their species, the long bill is specially adapted to sipping nectar from its chosen food plant.

The natural world's symbiotic relationships are nowhere better illustrated than between humming-bird and flower. The trumpet creeper (*Campsis radicans*) is native to the United States from Florida and Texas to New Jersey, where it enjoys moist woodland and wayside habitats, its brilliant red corolla designed to attract humming-birds, which pollinate the flower without damaging its tough, fleshy texture. This glorious partnership of bird and flower, colour and shape, movement and pattern is a gift to the embroiderer – imagination is eclipsed by reality (see Plate 1 on cover and page 2).

The trumpet creeper clings to brickwork and other supports by means of its long, ivy-like aerial roots – these I have slightly stylized by the use of finely couched gold thread. Its climbing stems, green and luxurious, which extend more than 9m (30ft) are crowned by clusters of bright flowers, crimson-orange as buds, opening into magnificent blooms – dark apricot at the throat and purple-red toward the lip. Lush, vibrant green leaves complete the picture. Pure, untwisted silk is a perfect choice for both humming-birds and creeper and, worked on black, the bright, almost luminescent colours are particularly effective.

Designed specifically with the jacket of this book in mind, the composition of

◁ *PLATE 41*
*The humming-bird's amazing agility results
from its unique physiology – the keel of its
breastbone is proportionally larger than that of
any other bird to support the massive flying
muscles which allow its wings to beat up to
eighty times a second. This produces the
droning hum which gives the bird its name –
like the frenetic flight of the bumble bee. In the
nineteenth century millions were killed to
support fashion's craze for feathered jewellery –
a fad which luckily died out before the birds
did! Rare birds and flowers (here the hibiscus)
are better captured in embroidery.*
14 x 19.25cm (5½ x 7¾in)

Plate 1 nevertheless comprises an accurate representation of the subject. There are times, however, when the loveliness of a certain combination of elements means that strictly correct interpretation is superseded by artistic licence. This wasn't the case with Plate 41 but was with Plate 42. Here, the rufous humming-bird is a marvellous confusion of colours from slate blue-grey to dusky green, brick orange to black and white. Not among the tiniest of its species, it is still vastly agile, able to fly up, down, sideways and even backward to position itself under its food-plants.

There are about one hundred species of the fuchsia genus, of which less than ten occur naturally outside Central and South America, and many are specifically adapted to pollination by humming-birds. *Fuchsia simplicicaulis* is an elementary member of the family (Fig 39), its long pendant flowers concealing rich and abundant nectar at the base. There are countless cultivars arising from the hybridization of early specimens brought to the Old World in the late eighteenth and early nineteenth centuries, of which 'Swanley Gem' (top of Plate 42), 'Citation'

HELEN M.
STEVENS

(middle) and 'Party Frock' (bottom) are only three. The juxtaposition of these flowers with the startling rufous humming-bird was irresistible.

Like many complex flowers, the key to working fuchsias successfully is to understand the anatomy of the bloom. The 'core' of the subject, back towards which all stitches must flow, is the ovary, the very centre of the flower from which the seeding body will develop. This occurs at the base of the petals, which are in turn protected by four long sepals (often mistaken for petals) which frame the flower and are frequently of a different shade. Radial and directional *opus plumarium* falls back toward the core, enhanced by shooting stitches on the petals, the long stamens, worked in straight and seed stitches, apparently disappearing into the throat of the flowers (see Fig 40). More comprehensive discussions of the anatomy of diverse flowers can be found in *Helen M. Stevens' Embroidered Flowers*.

Not all the jewels of the rain forest are nectar-sipping humming-birds: the predatory tyrant flycatchers constitute one of the largest of all families of perching birds. They are found only in the Americas and in many respects are similar to Old World flycatchers. The centre of the diversity of the family is in the Amazon basin, but the 370 species have spread wherever food is available, from Alaska to Tierra del Fuego. The many-coloured Rush-tyrant (*Tachuris rubrigastra*) (Plate 43) is one of the most exotic. As its name suggests, this fiercely territorial little bird inhabits swampy ground and meadows near water where it builds its intricately woven nest in reeds and grasses, particularly cats'-tails, up to 80cm (30in) above the water.

There are seven distinct colours visible in the plumage of this attractive bird, not to mention the graduation of shading! As ever, successive strata of radial *opus plumarium* fall back towards the core (beak), the stitches themselves blending smoothly, despite the sharp delineation of the markings. As one colour feeds into the next, allow the stitches to fall randomly, sometimes between, sometimes

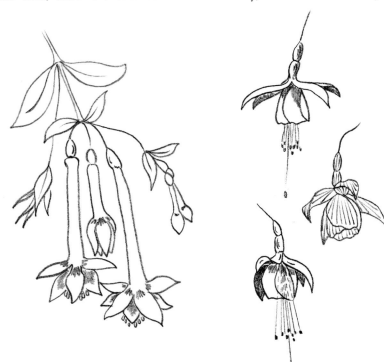

PLATE 43 ▷

Long, sinuous, gently curved outlines and motifs can be rendered in a number of ways, three of which are included here: snake stitch (large leaf blade to the right), narrow stem stitch (grasses) and couching, both single and multiple (tendrils).

In the first two of these techniques, the rule 'always bring your needle out *on the* outside *of the curve' allows the stitches to sweep smoothly in the direction of the overall curve, without 'fighting' it (see Appendix A and the Masterclass sections of* Helen M. Stevens' Embroidered Flowers *and* Embroidered Butterflies*). In couching, where a single metallic or other thread is held in place by a fine line of couching stitches, motifs can be broadened by bringing two or more of the base threads together, as shown toward the bottom of this study. Each base thread should be couched down individually, but, as the tendrils meet, should lie closely abutted.*

10 x 26.75cm (4 x 10½in)

HELEN M.
STEVENS

◁ *PLATE 44*
In terms of superlatives Cithaerias philis *is
certainly not the largest of tropical butterflies
(a mere 6.3cm/2¹⁄₂in) nor, subjectively, the most
beautiful (see Plate 62, page 107) but it is
certainly one of the most extraordinary. Most
butterflies rely upon their bright colouring to
attract mates, deter rivals and scare off
potential predators.* C. philis *would appear to
use none of these survival techniques. Apart
from the false eye-spots on the hind-wings,
which are so subdued as to be almost invisible,
their colours consist of a subtle translucent blush
graduating through several shades and which is
only evident when caught by the light.
Perhaps the transparency of their wings (so
successfully rendered with a cellophane thread)
is, indeed, a form of camouflage – there would
certainly seem to be no other explanation for
the evolution of such a fragile membrane. By
definition, in a rain forest the rain comes
frequently, suddenly and with a vengeance.
Delicate butterflies have only seconds to find
shelter or their wings may be torn to shreds by
a torrential downpour.*
10.25 x 23.5cm (4¹⁄₄ x 9¹⁄₄in)

through the stitches of the preceding strata. In this way the colours will merge abruptly, but each individual strata will be evenly integrated.

From humming-birds as tiny as bumble bees to butterflies larger than many birds, the rain forest is a riot of the unexpected. Deep in the South American interior live creatures yet to be identified by science – many of those which have been found still retain the mystery of their food-plants and life cycles. Such a genus is the cithaerias, a family of about ten species of butterfly which fly in the dark recesses of the forest. With transparent wings and pencil-slim bodies, these ethereal insects flash translucent shades of colour when caught by a rare, filtered shaft of sunlight: *Cithaerias philis* is suffused with violet (Plate 44). The shimmering, cellular effect of these wings is almost impossible to capture in photography; water-colour and oils can only suggest its fragile beauty. In embroidery, however, the extraordinary tissue-thin membrane can be brought to life.

The outer edge of each wing is worked in a narrow band of snake stitch and the golden-brown veins sketched in fine stem stitch. Where purple and violet shades glow on the lower wings, work strata of radial *opus plumarium* in very fine silk, falling back towards the body of the insect. Similarly, the distinctive eye spots towards the outer margins of the lower wings should be completed at this stage. Now we are ready to weave the magic! Using a blending filament (this comprises two twined threads, one silky, the other cellophane) separate out the cellophane strand. Thread this onto a fine needle (a beading needle is ideal) and work a single long strata of open radial *opus plumarium* superimposing the stitches over the underlying embroidery. There are a wide choice of colours available in blending filaments (see Suppliers, page 143) so shades may vary according to the needs of the subject. By choosing to work at least a portion of the wing over a background feature (such as the stem of the flower) the transparent effect is further enhanced.

Since the cithaerias has guarded the actual secrets of its life style so well, we are at liberty to choose any plant as its companion. Another subject which retains an aura of mystery is *Calliandra haematocephala* – the blood red powder-puff. This was first recorded in 1855 but as a cultivated plant grown from a seed sent to Java from Calcutta! Not until 1892 was a very similar plant discovered growing in the wild in Bolivia. It seems unlikely that this plant, known to grow wild in the New World, should also have evolved apparently separately in the Old, and so it is believed that some unknown explorer and plant lover brought a seed back to Europe in the eighteenth century, cultivars of which passed throughout the botanical establishment for decades without its true origin being known. Whatever its antecedents, however, it is a spectacular subject.

Simple pea-like leaves belie the complexity of the calliandra flower. The head consists of a multitude of florets, packed closely toward the core, sheathed in sepals which burst out of blackberry-like buds. Each floret contains four long stamens and an even longer style, tipped with a bead-like stigma. Floating embroidery is the perfect medium to capture this powder-puff effect. Worked in two shades of crimson and pink, the filaments intermingle to give an impression of shot silk, tiny seed stitches in gold metallic thread tipping the longer stitches.

▽ *Fig 41*
A meandering couched thread will need more couching stitches than one which is lying straight. Make sure that the main thread is anchored securely at each twist and turn of the design, particularly in the 'U' of the hairpin bends.

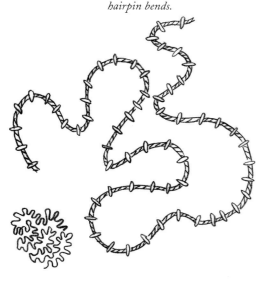

BRAVE NEW WORLD

In the late twentieth century the arrival upon the embroidery scene of a myriad of new and exciting threads and specialist decorative materials opened the stage door to a fresh dimension of inspiration and interpretation. As the millennium turns, startling and original art forms tempt us into cross-media experiments. This, of course, is nothing new: as far back as the eighth and ninth centuries embroidery design was influenced by other disciplines, from metalwork to illuminated manuscripts and architecture. The combination of traditional techniques, modern materials and futuristic concepts is compelling.

Ideas such as time-lapse and freeze-frame photography have been with us for some time – natural history studies would be the poorer without them – but the effects of laser shows and holograms are relatively unexplored in association with textiles. In this twenty-first century 'world of embroidery' we can look a little closer at how some of these embroidery/high-tech hybrids can be achieved and presented. I have chosen to explore a sequence of three small embroideries which together cover a wide spectrum of ideas, beginning with capturing the passage of time.

Plate 45 shows a small moth and butterfly – a traditionally night-flying and daylight-loving combination, although the peach blossom moth (*Thyatira batis*) is also diurnal. The evolution of night-time through dawn and into daylight (from the bottom left to top right) is suggested by a background fabric entirely filled with randomly couched blending filaments (Fig 41), graduating from midnight blue through the mauves of the early hours into the ice-blue, white and pink of the morning. The undivided filament is couched down with a very fine silk thread – which also needs to change shade as the work progresses to remain invisible. The moth and holly blue butterfly (*Celastrina argiolus*) worked first, are surrounded by the meandering design, their antennae finally superimposed over the couching. In this way the insects are an integral part of the overall pattern, neither dominant nor passive – simply a part of the progress of daybreak.

If several hours are caught in a single study in Plate 45, Plate 46 attempts to capture the nanosecond when tiny droplets of water fall from the petals of a pasque flower (*Pulsatilla vulgaris*) and erupt into miniature rainbows. If a moment of time is to be frozen, the finest details of the subject matter, too, must also be observed. The enchanting purple-violet pasque flower is rare in the wild (in Britain it grows only on dry, chalky grassland between Essex and Gloucestershire), but I have several plants in my garden which enable close inspection. The fleshy stalks

▽ *PLATE 45*
Multiple Dalmatian dog spotting on the wings of the peach blossom moth and the two fine strata of radial opus plumarium *along the outer margins of the holly blue's wings are the only regimented techniques in this otherwise very free study. The randomly meandering couching of the background is slightly angular – a result of the easily manipulated nature of the blending filament – and alternating lines of colour suggest the points of transition between dark and light. Large fields worked in this technique can be very effective in breaking down a background colour. It is worked on a black base in Plate 68 (page 116).*
8.25 x 8.25cm (3¼ x 3¼in)

PLATE 46 ▷

It is often forgotten that beneath the tough, shiny wing cases of most beetles are delicate structures as fine as those of mayflies and lacewings (see also the discussion with regard to the scarab beetle in Chapter Three). Long, straight, open radial work captures the movement of the wings in flight; short straight stitches suggest legs and antennae. Worked on this scale (as opposed to the larger ladybird study in Plate 37, page 65) the wing case spots are overlaid in studding and the more naturalistic style omits any gold thread or other embellishments.

10 x 10cm (4 x 4in) including mount

are covered with minute hairs, the effect replicated in the filigree of the sepals and upper leaves. The petals themselves are the texture of velvet, smooth and luxuriant, whilst at the centre of each flower is a cushion of bright yellow pollen-bearing stamens and a further cone of filaments, cream at their base and suffused with purple at the tip, like the wavering strands of a glass-fibre lamp.

The complexities of the plant can be interpreted in pure silk: snake stitch, the finest stem stitch to create the intricately segmented leaves, straight and seed stitches for the filaments and pollen-bearing mass, and radial and opposite angle *opus plumarium* for the flower. Tiny seed beads in transparent white and ice-blue suggest the water gathered at the centre of the left-hand flower, and rolling off the velvety surface of the petal to the right. The droplets are still entire as they almost reach the ground − only then do they explode into translucent bursts of pastel colour. Faceted, hyalescent sequins are caught to the background fabric with a cellophane thread. The flight of the seven-spot ladybird (*Coccinella 7-punta*) is rapid enough to jet between the two. Modern sequins, unlike their old metallic counterparts, will not deteriorate or tarnish. They are available in a wide range of shapes and sizes − some as tiny as the seed beads in Plate 46.

In Plate 47 I have tried to create the illusory effect of a hologram. The flat, unfaceted miniature sequins are interspersed with round beads, this dimensional diversity tricking the eye into interpreting the pattern on two levels. The silk-work

◁ *PLATE 47*
*A subtle graduation of the colours chosen for the
miniature sequins and seed beads in this study,
from very pale pastel shades at the top to duller
golden-browns at the base, is another device to
slightly confuse the logic of the eye! Whilst at
first glance these additions seem uniform, the
deepening shades appear to make the
arrangement denser toward the bottom of the
composition. This in turn gives the impression
that the mayfly is flying 'through' an altered
light source, adding to the holographic effect.*
12.75 x 12.75cm (5 x 5in) including frame

iris, its stem seen through the fine stitches of the mayfly's wing, continues the
impression of depth and movement. This is further enhanced by drawing the eye
into the study by displaying the piece within a window mount, itself framed by a
deep moulding, the frame picking out the blue shades of both mount and subject.

Obviously, the most important aspect of any presentation is the mounting of
the work onto its backing. This is fully discussed in Appendix B. The recreation for
display of the tension under which the embroidery was originally worked is essential
to show it at its best. A window mount (shown without a frame in Plate 45) is
always necessary if beads, sequins or other three-dimensional additions are
incorporated into the work and both this and the frame should be chosen to
enhance the subject rather than overwhelm it. There has been much debate in the
world of modern art embroidery as to the advantages of framing in reflective or
non-reflective glass. I feel that non-reflective glass tends to deaden colours and
slightly blur the outline of fine embroidery. It is not always easy to find a location
in which to display your work which avoids the reflection of windows and other
light sources, but remember that the light itself is an integral part of the
embroidery's overall effect. Keeping silks and other textiles away from direct
sunlight is important, but do not be afraid of good, directional lighting – in
particular, artificial light at night brings silk-work to life and a spotlight positioned
to recreate the light source by which the work was achieved is especially effective.

CHAPTER FIVE

CITY LIGHTS

You're weaving life into a mad jazz pattern
Ruled by Pantaloon!
Poor little rich girl,
Don't drop a stitch too soon.

Noel Coward
'Poor Little Rich Girl'

THE GREAT WHITE WAY

PLATE 49 ▷

The hothouse flower of the speak-easies, an orchid, in this case the magnificent cattleya species, 'Nellie Roberts'. This embroidery is worked throughout in a single strand of fine floss silk to allow the dense, velvety nature of the petals to separate successfully into the detailed, meandering indentations of their outer edges.

8.25 x 7.5cm (3¼ x 3in)

◁ *PLATE 48*

'Come on along and listen to the lullaby of Broadway' the lyrics of Al Dubin, music of Harry Warren and direction of the famous Busby Berkeley in Gold Diggers of 1935, *an incredible piece of black and white film fantasy, had a considerable influence over the creation of this embroidery. Hollywood musicals of the 1930s are a marvellous source of art deco inspiration – their restricted monochrome shading can teach us much about how to construct a dramatic picture with a limited palette of colours. The then favourite motion-picture device of the 'montage' can also be adapted to create startling effects.*

Here, I have used several different 'dimensions' of space to create the impression of the montage: the skyscrapers in the foreground, the distant city skyline, and the linking element of the bridge, each softened by the swirling mists of unspun silk. The black expense of sky is broken by the colours of dawn sweeping upward and to the left as the eye is returned to the foremost building: the circle is complete.

The Chrysler building is a curious combination of modern and gothic styles (see also Plate 53). At the base of the topmost sequence of towers there is a series of modernist gargoyles serving no other purpose than decoration.

See also the Dedication on page 4.

Embroidery shown life-size:
39.25 x 30cm (15½ x 11¾in)

· · · · · · · · ·

Perhaps more than any other universal style, the novelty of art deco lay in the fact that it was dominated by designers of fashion, and therefore to a large extent of the textile world. The ziggurats, cubic motifs and geometric, exaggerated interpretations of floral and foliate patterns, are to be found equally in the finest gauze handkerchief produced by a top Paris fashion house to the dizzy heights of New York's Empire State and Chrysler buildings. The clothes and accessories were worn by a new type of woman whose fresh-found independence had been hard won whilst the men were away fighting the Great War. Home furnishings were equally influenced by the ideals of this emancipated individual, and architecture followed.

Designers exploited the new elite's weakness for fashion by changing it on a regular basis – *haute couture* hemlines shot up and down like fever-charts and waistlines travelled too, from below the bust to below the navel. Certain colours became the signature of the 'It' girl, to be swiftly absorbed into wider acceptance of interior design: silver and black became the recognisable shades of a sophisticated home, together with others which emerged from the worlds of show business and night-clubs – 'tango' was a burnt orange which took its name from the popular (and some thought shockingly erotic) Latin dance of the American speak-easies.

Paris led the movement in the early 1920s, dominated by the couturiers (Fig 42) but in the mid-decade an unexpected influence came from Cairo as the discovery of Tutankhamen's tomb made the Egyptian look predominant for a while (Fig 44). By the 1930s, however, Broadway and then Hollywood became the ideals by which glamour-addicted middle classes set their standards. The lives of the stars of stage and screen, their clothes, homes, holidays and careers became obsessions. Film fan magazines explored every aspect of life-style design.

I have tried to capture the glamour and mysterious allure of contemporary New York at night in Plate 48. The dark waters of the river reflect the lights of the city that never sleeps, from the mists of the early dawn the skyscrapers thrust upwards into the still black sky, the red and gold contrails of fast-moving cars streak across the Hudson Bridge, itself suggested only by the invisibly suspended globes of streetlights.

A picture such as this presents a number of inherent challenges. The skyline needs to be suggested impressionistically – the reflections even more so – and yet the nearer buildings require an element of detail which must convey the architecture without getting bogged down with technical extrania. To the left is the Chrysler Building, the embodiment of American Deco and still a popular Big Apple landmark. It was designed by William van Alen, sometimes called 'the Zeigfield of his profession', and was faced entirely in nirosta, a material chosen by Walter P. Chrysler himself as it had an effect similar to platinum − show-biz and fashion were the combined ethos of the building. Rising to almost 320m (1,050ft), the multi-arched dome which tops the structure is perforated by triangular windows in an obscure homage to the pyramids, whilst futuristic gargoyles overhang the first 'step' of the widening base.

Worked in both floss and twisted silks, in shades of grey from silver to gunmetal, the building is 'floodlit' by blue blending filaments superimposed over the underlying straight dashing stitches (see Appendix A, page 129). Unlit windows are worked in black, to produce a still deeper contrast with the darkest of the grey stitching. To emphasize the metallic fascia, silver thread is couched along the outlines and into the voids of the main features of the building.

The Empire State Building, to the right, was completed (as was the Chrysler) in 1930. Much has been written about the supposed Aztec influences which produced the stepped-back architecture of many American skyscrapers. In fact, this was governed mainly by the zoning laws of 1916 which forbade towers rising in a solid mass to enormous heights: the taller the building the narrower the tower had to be in relation to the ground space occupied. The less elaborate architecture of the spire allows a more consistent use of dashing techniques in the embroidery, and again floodlighting is suggested by blending filaments in contrasting shades.

Simple, perpendicular dashing is used for the whole of the skyline, worked in both silver and black blending filaments and a two-stranded, twined black and gold silk thread. Specific arrangements of neon lights, such as on the arcaded jetty which juts into the water (centre), are suggested by seed stitches in gold metallic thread or high floss silk and the horizontal stitching which describes the water is interspersed with threads which match their counterparts above to create reflections.

The rising mist is unspun and undyed silk. Lifted straight from the cocoon at the first stage of production, the silk is naturally fluffy and light, and is teased into the various shapes shown. Its own static holds it to the background fabric and allows it to meander over underlying features. A similar technique is also used in Plate 2 (page 6, detail Plate 74, page 122).

Nature, or a highly cultivated and sophisticated version of it, could not escape the attention of the 'bright young things' and their gurus of the 1920s and 1930s. No evening engagement was complete without the delivery of a corsage (usually direct from an expensive, fashionable

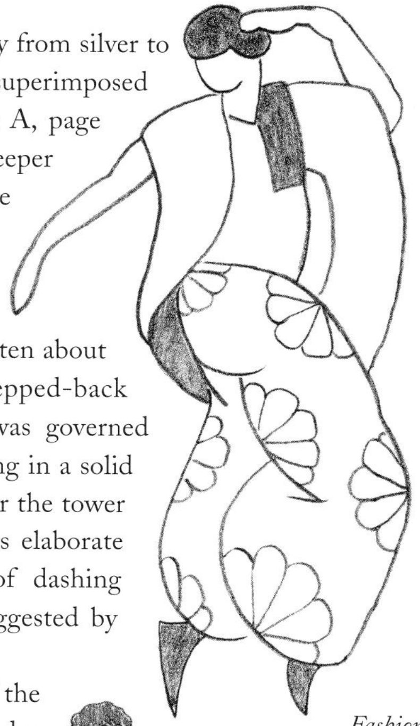

△ *Fig 42*
Fashion as art and art as fashion − in the world of art deco the two were indistinguishable. Short skirts and baggy pantaloons freed women from the restrictions of corsets, but the 'It' girl was now a slave to the passing fancies of the designers, and all else followed.

◁ *Fig 43*
Just as if our model were a flower and her gown its petals, analyze the flow of the fabric to achieve a realistic effect. The 'bustle' is gathered into the bow at the back of the dress: channel your stitches accordingly. The long, straight, tubular line of the bodice and skirt has no specific core other than the waistline, but imagine them hung on a clothes-hanger: angle your stitches as though the fabric was trying to fall back into its north/south alignment.

. . . .

florist): discreet pins and chains attached these hot-house blooms to delicate silk or filmy gauze dresses (Plate 49). New York's Radio City Music Hall opened in December 1932 with a seating capacity of 6,200. It contained thirty-one lounges and smoking rooms, each decorated in various 'modern' styles: the murals decorating the walls of the women's lounge on the first mezzanine are a series of fabulous natural studies by the Japanese artist Yasuo Kuniyoshi reminiscent of the screen-printed textiles of the earlier decades of the century. Huge lilies and sweeping, sinuous leaves echo the fashionable profile of the free and easy boy-girl with a cocktail glass, cigarette holder and jewelled bandeau (Plate 50).

Many designer and furnishing fabrics were produced in bold, exaggerated designs (Fig 44), though a single vibrant shade, flamingo-pink, bottle-green or kingfisher-blue could make a 'simple' cocktail gown appear more sophisticated than showy. A self-coloured model is also easier to render in embroidery (see Plate 50),

PLATE 50 ▷

McCall's fashion magazine of 1928 advised that fashionable young women filled the bustles of their evening gowns with tissue paper of the same colour as the fabric '. . .you know the trick by the crackle of the paper as they sit down'.

Patterns for outfits such as this could be acquired from McCall for around 45 US cents. A rapidly diminishing clientele able to afford couturier's prices made the mass production of patterns profitable, and embroidery designs suitable for working onto such elegant creations also became available. The 'gamin' look – in America she was called 'the Flapper', in Italy 'la Maschietta' *and in France* 'la Garçonne' *– decreed the disappearance of the bust, allowing a perfect opportunity for embroidered decoration uninterrupted by cleavage!*

The bobbed hair is worked in fine straight stitching, interspersed with black to suggest the body and 'fall' of the new, razor-edged style.

The skin is in fine speckling stitch (see Chapter Seven) subtly shaded toward the underside of each feature.

9.5 x 10.25cm (3³/₄ x 8in)

Long, dangling necklaces were a vital accessory during the 1920s and went well with the flat-fronted look. Here, a pendant is worked in the design of a winter aconite (a naturally angular flower) on lightly padded flamingo-pink silk. Clockwise around the central compact case is a pill-box decorated with a butterfly motif, a silk evening bag decorated by a twisted cord and embroidered grasshopper, a cyclamen brooch incorporating tiny seed beads and cufflinks showing a 'jazz-age' motif of interlaced initials and musical notes. Top left is a notebook embellished with a vibrant green beetle. Insect designs were popular, possibly inspired by sacred scarab beetles (see Plate 36, page 65) originally made fashionable by the excavation of Tutankhamen's tomb. To the right, a picture frame is decorated with a snowdrop motif.
Compact case 7cm (2³⁄₄in) round;
cufflinks 1.8cm (³⁄₄in) high

allowing the sweep and fall of the fabric to be emphasized without the confusion of a complex pattern. By treating the low, dropped waist of the outfit as the 'core' of the stitching, directional *opus plumarium* sweeps down on the bodice and up on the skirt, converging at the bow on the 'bustle' of the dress. Careful shadow lining delineates the folds of the fabric and where its underside is revealed a deeper shade is used throughout. Otherwise, the changes of colour are minimal and mainly created simply by the changing flow of the stitches (Fig 43).

Accessories were *de rigueur* in this maelstrom of city life. Evening bags, compacts, powder and trinket boxes, notebooks and jewellery: no element of personal necessity escaped the influence of the designers. We can use something of this passion in creating miniature embroideries of our own – embroideries which can be with us everyday. Plate 51 shows a collection of such small items. When working embroideries for specific purposes, it is important to bear certain practicalities in mind. Silk, or any other textile which is intended for everyday use, if it is to last undamaged, should be protected if possible. On a compact (centre), pill-box, pendant, brooch or even cuff-links, this is usually easily achieved by the purchase of an item already supplied with such protective covering. There are a number of companies producing high quality goods perfect for the display of even the finest embroidery (see Suppliers). Items which, by their very nature, will be handled directly, such as a notebook or evening bag (top left and right) should be stored, when not in use, in acid-free tissue paper.

△ *Fig 44*

Top: The stylized open wings and body of a scarab beetle, art deco style (see also Fig 32). Bottom: Fashionable resorts such as Cuba and the West Indies began to influence designs of all kinds.

PAST GLORIES

The dictates of fashion, whether personal or on a grander scale are nothing new. In the cities of medieval Europe high society was as obsessed by the current fads and fancies of dress and design as their descendants. Italy and France, then as now, were seen as the trend setters. In fourteenth century Venice, carnivals and masques were an excuse to indulge in both personal and public excesses of behaviour and fashion, but even everyday life at the Doge's Palace was lived in an atmosphere of intrigue and drama: a richly woven silk tapestry of vice and velvet, poison and pearl-encrusted nets to snare the unwary plotter. In the *Masque of the Red Death*, Edgar Allan Poe sets the scene perfectly:

> *. . .velvet tapestries hung all over the ceiling and down the walls, falling in heavy folds upon a carpet of the same material. And thus were produced a multitude of gaudy and fantastic appearances. . . it was a gay and magnificent revel.*

PLATE 52 ▷
'Paint must never hope to reproduce the faint Half-flush that dies along her throat'.
When Robert Browning (1812–1889), a long-term resident of Venice, together with his wife and fellow poet, Elizabeth Barrett, wrote My Last Duchess *he could unwittingly have been describing the effect of the medieval split stitch, widely used in English embroidered portraiture during the Anglo-Saxon period. Working in a single strand of fine silk allows the subtlest graduation of shades in the flesh tones, from a pale rosy-pink on the cheek bone to a shadowed blush beneath the eyebrows and chin and on the neck. By analyzing the structure of the face to remind you of the ultimate flow of the stitches a close-up portrait such as this can become amazingly life-like.*
10cm (4in) diameter, including frame

Plate 52 is inspired by the riches of medieval city life. During the fourteenth century the hair of a mature woman was often completely hidden by an elaborate head-dress. Fashions were frequently upshots of unfortunate necessity – the plague could severely affect the scalp but hair loss could, at least, be disguised. Silk, velvet, cloth-of-gold, precious stones, pearls, gold and silver were everyday wear among the ruling classes, and here I have tried to recreate a little of that abundance of wealth. The flesh tones of the face and neck are worked in silk in very fine split stitch (a technique which was used in religious and other embroidery during the early Middle Ages), following the natural contours of the features, discreet shadow lining and shading emphasizing the shape (see Fig 45, and for a full discussion of working facial features, see *The Timeless Art of Embroidery*). Pure silk in a slightly thicker gauge is used for the white kerchief framing the forehead and at the nape of the neck, whilst a still thicker gauge suggests the dense velvet of the main head-dress. This is worked in directional *opus plumarium*, establishing the flow of the fabric around the head, and to each side is overlaid with a finely couched gold thread, seed beads caught down at each intersection of the 'net'. The jewelled cloth-of-gold band is created by working tiny fields of brightly coloured silk to suggest the gems, surrounded by broadly directional *opus plumarium* (voided) and outlined in a double, couched, real gold thread.

A brocaded cord borders the gown. This is worked in fine snake stitch, whipped with a fine gold thread, the necklace individually stitched faux seed pearls. Finally, two real amethysts for the pendant and brooch are held in place by adapted shisha stitching (see page 58), the glow of crystal completing the overall richness of the composition. Set in a miniature frame, the portrait is protected by a domed glass which stands proud of the three-dimensional beads and stones.

For centuries the cathedral of Notre-Dame at Rheims in Champagne was the coronation church of French royalty. The strictly regimented customs of life at the Cardinal Lord Archbishop's Court are rendered, tongue-in-cheek, in the wonderful poem by Thomas Ingoldsby, *The Jackdaw of Rheims*, during which, as the Cardinal attends to his personal ablutions using 'the best white diaper, fringed with pink', a saucy jackdaw steals his ring. The jackdaw's hilarious penance, confession and final absolution and the brilliant description of medieval life made this a childhood favourite of mine, and Plate 53 is my tribute.

The cathedral spire, like the towering bulk of the Chrysler Building in Plate 49, is worked in floss, gunmetal-grey silk (the actual, rather uninspiring twin towers of Rheims seemed somehow less attractive!), long radial *opus plumarium* worked toward the apex of the spire and needlewoven through with a contrasting grey. The gold decoration is worked in couched metallic thread, augmented by seed stitches at regular intervals. Below, the main body of the building and the multi-directional roofs are worked in etching, dashing and straight stitches (see Fig 46), fading away toward the base of the study, where the Preacher's Cross stands above the invisible city market-place. On a twisted hemp rope the jackdaw surveys the scene of his crime, ring in beak.

The jackdaw (*Corvus monedula*) is a sociable little crow, much given to human contact and infamous for its habit of 'borrowing' shiny objects to hoard in its nest. Arriving from nowhere, a jackdaw took up residence with me for a couple of years, during which time it became so brash as to come into the kitchen and appropriate teaspoons and bottle tops. One day 'Jack' disappeared as suddenly as he had arrived,

△ *Fig 45*
With the light source from the top right quadrant, shadows will fall below overhanging features such as the head-dress, chin and fringe. This ornate design could be presented similarly to the miniature in Plate 52 and/or as a companion piece to the male portrait in Fig 25, page 55.

△ *Fig 46*
The roofs of medieval towns and cities are a joy for lovers of architecture and art. Juxtaposed angles, deep shadows, reflections and textures all come together. Fine detail is not necessary if the basic structures are etched in correctly, firmly and with confidence.

PLATE 53 ▷

Whilst birds of paradise and humming-birds naturally present a spectacular range of effects to the embroiderer, there is something to be said for occasionally taking on the challenge of an unlikely, some might say, unapproachable subject. On a bird which is almost uniformly black, save for his rather dour monk's hood, where does one begin to find life and movement in a jackdaw? Firstly, in the pose of the subject: forget those dull mug-shot profiles in most field guides, a turn of the head and a jaunty stance makes all the difference. This need not be as difficult to achieve as you may imagine. The sweep of the stitches, flowing along a fluid Z-bend, catch and refract the light on the handsome black and grey plumage with a military dash to rival any tropical interloper.

15.25 x 35cm (6 x 9in)

PLATE 54 (far right) ▷

The inclusion of an unexpected shade to an otherwise predictable palette of colours can lift a piece of work to unusual effects. Among the silver-blues and greens and the flinty stonework I have incorporated the occasional flash of mauve – a tree catching a shaft of moonlight or a clump of grasses emerging from the shadows. There is also a slight pinkness to the silver of the moon. The long, angled cellophane threads suggest that the moonbeams disappear off the edge of the picture to the right. When framed, these should be allowed similarly to vanish under the window mount. This technique is discussed in detail in The Myth and Magic of Embroidery.

21.5 x 12.75cm (8½ x 5in)

but his cocky 'jizz' and cheeky blue eyes have remained in my memory. Apart from the silver-grey monk's cowl at the nape of the bird's neck, and a blue-grey sheen to his underparts, the jackdaw is entirely black. To shadow line individual primary and secondary feathers would be ineffectual, but a void left between these features (as if on a black background) breaks up the otherwise uniform plumage. The sweep of the stitches converge smoothly toward the beak and the outline is softened by a narrow outer strata in fine silk to suggest the slightly fluffier feathers of the legs and belly.

A favourite nesting site for jackdaws is in old church towers, belfries and ruins but its comic antics, quick, agile flight and cheerful, explosive call, 'crackerjack!' has not cursed it with the doom-laden reputation of other crows such as the raven or

◁ *Fig 47*
Taking the centre of the full moon as the source of the light, establish the fields of the moonbeams by drawing a bead from that point, through the upper and lower extremities of the ruined windows or other defining structures, and on out of the perimeter of the picture. Within the arcs created, work long radial stitches in clear cellophane thread behind features to the front of the apertures and before features to the rear of them, allowing the stitches to converge as they reach their source (the moon). When presenting the finished piece, make sure a window mount covers the outer edges of the moonbeams, as they appear to 'flood' out of the picture.

carrion crow. Many a medieval abbey ruin (the heart of dozens of thriving small-city communities were ripped out during the English Reformation of the sixteenth century) boasts a colony of jackdaws. Perhaps my Jack made his way back to the abbey ruins of Bury St Edmunds in Suffolk, my local market town.

By day, the tourists flock to the remains of what was once the most important shrine in England – the burial place of St Edmund, martyred in 869 and the patron Saint of England until replaced by St George during the time of the Crusades. At night, especially in the winter, the ruined walls and arches are a place of moonlit magic, a silent mystery in the midst of busy town night-life (Plate 54). In this small landscape I have used only seed and straight stitches to convey the contrasting textures of masonry and tree, another picture predominantly worked in grey and white, but full of interest and detail. Long straight-stitched cellophane strands suggest moonbeams, the light catching the upper and left-hand features of the ruins as they pass. It can be useful to make a shorthand 'note' at the sketch-book stage of a design such as this to remind yourself of the directional light-flow (see Fig 47). The trees are worked from trunk to twig in progressively finer threads, while touches of lilac in the grasses enhance the ethereal moonlight – the glow is caught in very pale pink quartz crystals nestling at the foot of the curtain wall.

FORBIDDEN CITY

It would be impossible to compile any book, however personal, attempting to capture a spirit of the 'world' of embroidery without mentioning China and its long and fascinating tradition of textile art. Chinese embroidery forms such a huge corpus of work, its execution reached heights of such immaculate skill, and so much has been written on the subject that most appropriate superlatives have already been used elsewhere! Just as it has often been argued that it is wrong to compromise the integrity of embroidery by attempting to make it imitate other art forms, so it would seem presumptuous to 'interpret' Chinese techniques and styles in radical ways. We can but sit at the feet of the masters and, hopefully, expand our appreciation.

Fig 48 ▷
The Silk Route – beginning in China and encompassing almost the whole of the ancient world – its very name conjures up romance and adventure. In fact, it was made up of a number of trading roads which carried silk, spices and slaves across Asia and beyond. Fully established a century or so before the Christian era, ports in the Mediterranean exported commodities to western Europe and all the Roman Empire.

The Chinese were the first to learn the secrets of spinning and weaving silk and had dye workshops as early as 3000BC, although the secrets of sericulture were always jealously guarded. The silk was exported along the famous 'silk route' (Fig 48). The rich tradition which we have come to think of as 'Chinese embroidery'

truly reflects more the cultural influences of the Imperial Court of Peking – the Forbidden City – than the diverse geographical regions of this enormous country. The most characteristic type of embroidery was worked in the Imperial workshops before the Revolution of 1911, a tradition which can be traced back centuries (Fig 49). Satin stitch (sometimes double-sided, in which pictures were worked by two embroiderers sitting either side of a vertical frame producing no 'reverse'), Peking stitch (a form of interlaced back stitch), and the 'forbidden knot' were all favourite filling techniques (Fig 50). Voiding and couching added to the diversity of effect. Symbolism played an important part in design.

Dragons are popular motifs in Chinese embroidery, benevolent creatures in oriental lore, and supreme in their hierarchy is the five-clawed *lung* dragon (Plate 55). Several Manchu emperors decreed that only they and their immediate families were allowed to wear the *lung* dragon – less aristocratic dynasties had to unstitch one claw from each foot of existing embroideries! The four-clawed *mang* dragon could be worn by those outside the royal family, but (possibly my favourite), the *ch'ih* was only used on children's clothes – a friendly, one-horned, paddy-pawed dragon (Fig 51).

A dragon miniature is a delightful project. In Plate 55 I have simplified the design of the *lung* slightly, whilst retaining the coiling blue smoke of his breath and the traditional 'flaming jewel' motif which he pursues. A broad snake stitch is used on the sweeping neck and body, with the facial features picked out by voiding. Without attempting to imitate the richness of the Imperial embroideries, the dragon still retains the lively sense of movement and joviality so characteristic of the genre. Worked in floss silk with added gold and silver couched thread, the embroidery makes a vibrant contrast to its black background and is mounted in a small, fob-topped silver frame.

Also on black, Plate 56 contains further stylistic tributes to the tradition of Chinese embroidery. Symbolically, the crane (usually the white crane) represented long life and was a messenger of the gods. Within the Forbidden City, pleasure gardens and aviaries contained many birds and it is not impossible that the exotic crowned crane (*Balearica pavonina*) was a contemporary of several dynasties. I have chosen it for the startling contrast of white plumage against the black, and its splendid yellow-gold crown, colours echoed in its tail plumage. Chinese landscapes favour a natural composition of water, land and sky, each element an individual yet integrated part of the whole. I have tried to maintain this balance in my design, splitting the picture (roughly) into thirds horizontally. The water element from the base of the design to the skyline is dominated by the wading legs of the crane, and the reflected grasses; the 'land' is from the skyline to the top of the crane's head,

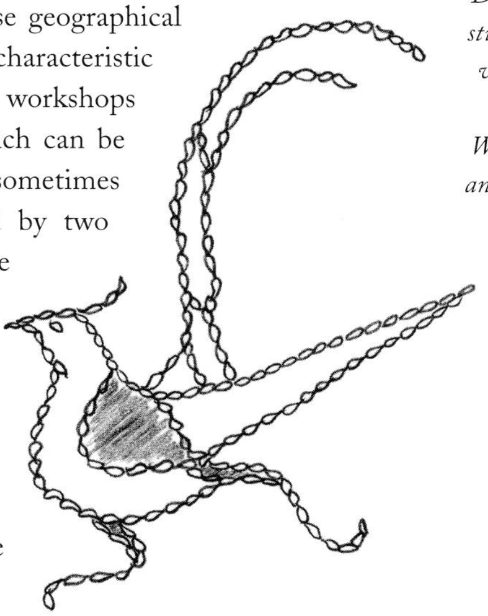

◁ *Fig 49*
Dating from the fifth century BC *this chain-stitched partridge motif worked in and on silk was found in an aristocratic tomb of around the period known as the Dynasty of the Warring States. With a golden body and tail and red legs, wing, beak and plumage, it is in a remarkably good state of repair – testament to the skills of the earliest embroiderers whose work remains extant.*

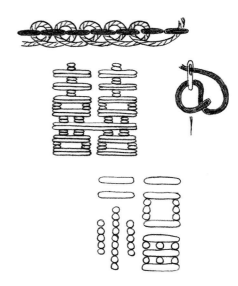

△ *Fig 50*
Top: Peking stitch – a looped border is formed by back stitch interlaced with a second thread, often in another colour.
Right: The 'forbidden' Peking knot.
Centre: The 'double felicity' character of Chinese calligraphy, symbol of conjugal happiness, often worked in parallel satin stitch.
Bottom: The fu *symbol of prosperity composed of straight stitch and Peking knots.*

Fig 51 ▷
The ch'ih *dragon, with lion's paws, in pursuit of the pink bat of happiness. Details like whiskers are not just a whimsy on my part – they do appear in traditional designs*

PLATE 56 (far right) ▷
A first-ranking civil official wore a crane (usually white) or a golden pheasant as his emblem of status and office. A p'u-tzu *similar to her husband's denoting his, and therefore also her, social standing would be worn by his wife. This might be in the form of a stylized landscape incorporating the bird or animal of rank – both civilian and military hierarchy was denoted by a variety of real and mythological beasts from flycatchers to unicorns and rhinoceros – or an elaborate confusion of symbolic devices. More formalized designs included characters of Chinese calligraphy (see Fig 50) but it was unusual for an embroiderer to sign his or her work.*
15.75 x 19.75cm (6¼ x 7¾in)

decorated by the fir tree, and the sky is from the top of the tree to the apex of the design. The three elements are strung together by the weeping tree.

Unlike Japanese design, in which large expanses of 'nothing' balance strong motifs, Chinese work usually appears more evenly distributed over its background. We can learn a great deal by looking at how various cultures 'balance' their pictures: the juxtaposition of elements can create distinctive and atmospheric effects without the addition of further fussy outlines.

PLATE 55 ▷
The 'flaming jewel' (bottom left) pursued by the dragon is a favourite motif in Chinese costume design. Court dress was formal: hip-length waistcoats (for both men and women) had front openings and were embroidered front and back, either directly onto the garment, or more especially since the Ming dynasty (1368–1644), onto p'u-tzu *or 'Mandarins' squares'. These 'squares' were often rectangular or, indeed, round; pairs of embroideries were worked as panels, one attached to the back of the waistcoat and the other, split down the middle before embroidery began, to either side of the front opening. On a larger scale, this design would have been typical for a member of the Imperial family.*
7.5cm (3in) diameter including frame

CHAPTER SIX

THE HIGH COUNTRY

Beyond the islands was the shining enamelled sea,
And beyond it again the rearing bulk of. . .
Plum coloured-distances embroidered
With threads and scrolls of snow.

Gavin Maxwell
Ring of Bright Water

HELEN M. STEVENS

PURPLE-HEADED MOUNTAINS

Some of the world's most beautiful flowers are to be found in its least accessible quarters. Given mankind's proclivity for over-exploitation, this is perhaps one of nature's defences, and whilst the impenetrable depths of the rain forest protect shelter-loving species, many sun- and light-worshipping plants are saved by their precipitous habitats. The gauzy shrouds of mountain mists are often embroidered with sparkling gems of vibrant wildflowers; in the Cape Province of South Africa the dense white clouds that hang about the summit of Table Mountain during the summer – known locally as the 'table cloth' – hide the spectacular beauty of orchids, irises and gladioli (Plate 57).

Exotic flowers offer us the opportunity to use colours which might otherwise lie undisturbed in our embroidery boxes for years. Those of us who enjoy temperate climates are used to the pastels and 'bright simples' of our native flora: the soft pinks of spring blossoms, dusty mauves and blues of high summer and startling true reds, yellows and whites of poppies and daisies. Begin to explore the plant life of different climates and (as we have seen with the 'new worlds') fresh vistas of colour and shape begin to open up before us. The very names of many of these species lead us into a world of high adventure, mythology and the stuff of Victorian novels. Like Ayesha, 'She Who Must be Obeyed', Rider Haggard's deathless queen of a lost African empire, Disa was a queen of antiquity and legend. Commanded to come before the King of Sweden 'neither naked nor dressed', she appeared draped in a fishing net. The early Victorian plant gatherers who 'discovered' *Disa uniflora* (second left in Plate 57) were reminded of this tale by the net-like tracery on the petals of this startling, crimson-red orchid. In the mid-nineteenth century it bordered every stream on Table Mountain, braving temperatures which dropped below freezing at night and rose to over 90°F (30°C) during the day.

Disa is cloaked in a mantled upper petal which protects its lower body. Against a creamy, fleshy ground, the inner surface of this petal is shot through with a geometric interlace of fine red thread-like veins – the 'net' of its namesake – which appears ready to fall forward over the pollen-bearing centre of the flower. The lateral petals echo this tracery with a more subtle pattern against their blood-red base. These two types of patterning should be approached differently. The dominant veins of the upper petal should be worked first in fine stem stitch, with radial and directional *opus plumarium* flooded around them. Shooting stitches (see Appendix A, page 127) are then worked into the *opus plumarium* in a paler red, the whole then being overlaid with straight stitches at right angles to the veins, completing the netted effect. This order of working is set out in Fig 52. The lower petals are worked in two strata of radial *opus plumarium* (the first a very short strata in cream), subsequently shot through with pale red and an occasional strand of cream. Where the inner features reflex, work opposite angle stitching, and overlay the central lip with tiny seed stitches.

To the left of disa in Plate 57, the cardinal red and white flower and buds of *Gladiolus cardinalis* describe a second elegant arc. Now rare in more accessible areas due to over-collecting, this delicate flower has adapted by colonising the mountains' most hard-to-reach locations. The flowers have the ability to adapt to strange situations – they can hang upside-down on a ledge, the stalk pendulous, but the blooms always upright as the large red petal remains uppermost by swivelling around in relation to its stem. Gladioli were named in acknowledgement of the spear-like shape of the budding flower head (like the short-handled sword of the Roman gladiators) and the plant's sharp lanceolate leaves. The buds open sequentially, lower flowers first, and when closed should be worked in progressive strata of radial *opus plumarium*, each strata falling back to the individual bud's core – the growing point at the base of each prospective flower.

Far right is shown one of the world's most spectacular flowers, the literally iridescent blooms of *Moraea villosa* (syn. *Moraea pavonia*), the Peacock Flower. Growing to a height of about 46cm (18in), the markings of the flower have a shimmering effect thought to be produced by a mingling of its unique blue sap and yellow cells in the petal tissue of the corolla (perianth). This creates an 'eye' – similar to the false eyes often found on the wings of butterflies (see Fig 53). The complicated patterning of the petals, together with the complex white and copper inner structures protecting the pollen masses, are worked entirely in radial *opus plumarium*. Blend each successive colour smoothly, but allow a sharp edge to the delineation of each strata, tailoring the length of your stitching to the depth of the respective field.

The leaves of each of these species are worked in long sinuous flows of snake stitch, or, where there is a central vein to the leaf, in sharply angled directional *opus plumarium*. Simple grasses are suggested by long, slightly angled straight stitches, contrasting with the horizontal straight stitches of the water and distant mountains (see caption to Plate 57).

From a flower named after a bird, the peacock, we turn to a butterfly named for a flower – the yellow pansy butterfly (*Junonia hierta*). It is easy to see how the name came into being: the insect's wings are blotched with yellow and mauve-blue, the natural colours of the European wild viola, the heartsease from which hybrid pansies were developed (see Fig 54). This widespread species is found from Africa via Arabia to Asia, the adult butterflies visiting a number of nectar-rich flowers to feed, but breeding on various members of the acanthus family (see Chapter Two). Though striking, this butterfly is simple to work, large Dalmatian dog spots smoothly merging into the black base field which is then ticked through to create the smaller markings.

A flower which can lay claim to being one of the world's highest-blooming species is a member of the poppy (*Papaveraceae*) family. *Meconopsis horridula* (Plate

▽ *Fig 52*
The 'standard' is the only complicated feature in the otherwise relatively simple disa. From the top, clockwise:
1 Outline of whole flower, without the interference of markings.
2 Dominant veins worked in stem stitch.
3 Radial and directional opus plumarium *flooded around the veins and shooting stitches added.*
4 Straight stitches worked at right angles to the underlying work.
5 Lower petals and other features completed in radial and opposite angle stitching as appropriate.

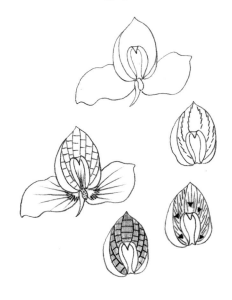

△ *Fig 53*

The Peacock Flower has long, sinuous petals alternated with rounded petals, both sporting five distinct strata of colour. The complex pollen mass at the flower centres obscures some areas of colour so work this first and flood the main strata around it, voiding between the two to keep them distinct and on two separate 'planes'.

58) has been recorded at altitudes up to 5,800m (19,000ft), its uppermost verified limit high on the slopes of Mount Everest. Despite its less than attractive name, this species of Himalayan poppy is one of its most lovely, ranging in colour from pale powder-blue to deep gentian. At the heart of each flower is a fine halo of golden stamens which, with the petals, fall away to reveal an elegant bottle-shaped fruiting body. Simple radial and directional *opus plumarium*, with overlaid seed stitching, describes this plant perfectly – techniques which can also be used on familiar European species such as the meadow cranesbill (*Geranium pratense*) in Plate 59.

The Himalayan range of mountains has proved to be not only a bastion against some of the most determined plant hunters, but also a barrier protecting the ethnic embroidery traditions of the north Indian sub-continent against the incursion of outside influences from western and central Asia. The Chamba district of Himachal Pradesh lies between the Punjab and Kashmir to the south-west of the Himalayas. It retains a unique tradition of embroidery known as the *rumal*. This is a square or rectangular narrative embroidery, usually bordered with a stylized floral or foliate design, the central panel spanning a variety of themes, from the war-like to festive or domestic scenes. Worked on a cotton ground in satin or back stitch, these panels can suggest an intriguing new dimension of design.

△ *Fig 54*

The delicate wild heartsease (Viola tricolor) from which modern garden pansies have been bred is a close relative of the long-spurred pansy (Viola calcarata) right, which grows at altitudes up to 2,130m (7,000ft) throughout the Alps and Apennines. The development of the pansy as a cottage garden favourite began in the early nineteenth century.

◁ *Fig 55*
A rumal *border, featuring convolvulus flowers, buds and foliage. This could be worked either as a border to be mounted separately and then overlaid on another piece of work, or simply as a framing feature for any other subject of your choice. Figs 16 and 32 (pages 37 and 64) would both fit the aperture to create interesting blends of ancient, modern, stylized and naturalistic.*

Based on the border of a traditional *rumal*, I have worked a square of interlaced tracery to surround a small embroidery (see Plate 59 and Fig 55) and mounted it separately onto a window-cut backing board. The 'narrative' panel itself tells a simple tale of the summer wayside – a bumble bee seeks nectar from a meadow cranesbill – but the composition is lifted from the commonplace into the exotic by the silk and gold framework around it. Don't be afraid to experiment with the traditions of other cultures to expand your own creativity.

BLUE REMEMBERED HILLS

Ice-blue lapping waters, the steely grey of the blue heron, silver fur, deep, immobile gunmetal reflections and the soft, rolling shapes and shades of the distant Rockies: a view from the eastward coastline of Vancouver Island (Plate 60) is a study of blue upon blue, the profile and colours of the mountains softened by distance.

I spent a large proportion of my childhood in North America and well remember family vacations, bowling along great inter-state highways while the seemingly endless range of the Rocky Mountains stretched ever further along the horizon, becoming infinitesimally larger as the miles were eaten up. My interests had not turned in the direction of textiles at that time, but at the age of six, great

◁ *PLATE 59 (opposite)*
The white-tailed bumble bee (Bombus lucorum) is a familiar visitor to members of the geranium family – like poppies, one of the most diverse groups of flowering plants. Mauve striations lead the bee to the nectar-rich pollen mass at the centre of the plant, and, dusted with pollen, it moves onto the next flower, fertilizing each as it visits. When the petals drop the descriptively named 'cranesbill' seed pod is left behind.
10 x 10cm (4 x 4in) including mount

HELEN M.
STEVENS

Fig 56 ▷
Giving a child a sketch-book and a few soft pencils can change their lives. After North America my family moved to the wilds of the Shetland Islands, far to the north of Scotland. During the 1960s the landscape was virtually unchanged after centuries of crofting, pony breeding, shepherding, spinning and knitting. In Unst (the northernmost island, and home for two years) I, armed with my crayons, first became aware of the interplay of animal and landscape.

◁ *PLATE 60*
The elegant, feathery plumes on the head of the heron only develop when the bird is mature – younger specimens resemble their parents, but until sexually active (like many crested birds) these display features are missing. The staple diet of most herons is fish, supplemented, depending upon their location, by eels, frogs and even small mammals such as (in Europe) water voles. The young sea otter, however, has nothing to fear – from the heron, at least. Securely clasped to its parent's tummy, oil spills and other pollution are now the greatest threat to survival.
This design is based upon threes: three main centres of interest (mountains, otters and foreground), each predominant feature roughly triangular. The framing feature of the heron takes the eye in three directions (see text).
Embroidery shown life-size:
39.25 x 25.5cm (15½ x 10in)

swathes of cheap paper were filled with scribblings of mountains, rocky foothills and sheer, precipitous drops (Fig 56) – not to mention my real passion, cowboys and Indians!

Many years later, when I was commissioned to work this embroidery of the view across the watery straits toward British Columbia the memories came flooding back: the mountains were old friends. As in Plate 57, the landscape features of this picture are worked entirely in straight horizontal stitching. The advantages of this technique for distant features, as well as the forward-sweeping middle ground, are several. Firstly, by maintaining a strictly horizontal direction to the work, the eye is led *across* the canvas, suggesting a broad, sweeping vista. Secondly, both the smooth blending of colours (Plate 57) and the abrupt change of shades, interrupted by voiding to suggest a break in the field of the perspective (Plate 61, detail of Plate 60) can be effected whilst still retaining an overall continuity to the stitching. Finally (and certainly not to be overlooked in working a large canvas) horizontal stitching allows for the use of very long, uninterrupted single stitches – up to 25cm (10in) – which means that the work builds up with surprising speed.

It is essential when working this type of 'impressionist' embroidered landscape that your background fabric is held tautly in its frame. My own preference (see Appendix B, page 135) is for a tambour hoop. Free-standing quilters' tambours can be up to 66cm (26in) across, ideal for large landscape work, giving a uniform tension, not only north, south, east and west, but also all points of the compass in between. If the tension of the work is correct at this stage it can be more easily recreated during the mounting process (Appendix B, page 138).

A heron in flight is unmistakable – its long neck tucked into its shoulders, the extravagant and steady wing beats making the most of any slight thermal, its feet visible behind the body (Fig 57). The blue heron (*Ardea herodias*) is equally as striking at rest. Long, featherless legs, ideal for striding through the shallows, are also sure-footed among rocks and rock-pools: a heron will stand motionless for long periods before making a sudden thrust with its spear-sharp beak, skewering its prey before deftly flipping it around to allow easy swallowing. The main, streamlined body feathers of heron should be worked (naturally) in smooth strata of radial *opus plumarium*, falling toward the beak, Dalmatian dog spotting and ticking creating the progressively more delicate markings on the breast and throat. An elongated fringe of feathers frame the speckles of the breast, which should be worked in overlaid straight stitches, their angle slightly at variance with the underlying work to give emphasis to this distinctive feature. In Plate 60 the heron forms a tri-corn border to the right of the landscape, the angles of beak and legs focusing the eye of the viewer toward the rest of the 'action' within the picture.

◁ *Fig 57*

Herons in flight. Several splendid herons have made their home in the nature reserve almost literally on my doorstep. Their rather ponderous flight is, nevertheless, elegant – these studies would make good subjects on which practise the techniques of miniaturization discussed on page 49, Fig 23.

Sea otters have been discussed fully in Chapter One. In Plate 60, the detail shown in Plate 17, page 30 is seen in relation to its full setting. Sea kelp (*Macrocystis*) swirls in fronds around the mother and baby otter, a vital part of their lives. Kelp forests form naturally off the western coasts of the Americas and have become a valuable commercial crop, used in a variety of food and pharmaceutical products. Sea otters act as aquatic forest rangers in the kelp beds which are their home – they rest in its canopy, give birth on beds made from its leathery leaves, anchor themselves to its stems to mate and play and, most importantly, feed on the sea urchins which can destroy a kelp forest like rabbits can ravage a lettuce bed. Apart from its commercial uses, sea kelp is a vital habitat for many animals. Charles Darwin wrote in 1834, 'The number of living creatures of all Orders, whose existence intimately depends upon the kelp is wonderful'. This is still true. Only the very top of the plant breaks through the surface of the water – Plate 60 shows the belt-like straps of the upper fronds arcing in and out of the ripples like sea serpents. By breaking up the colour of the water into darker shades with white highlights, movement is suggested: the fronds themselves are worked in swathes of directional *opus plumarium*.

PLATE 61 (detail of Plate 60) ▷
The voiding which differentiates one plane from the next on the mountains themselves is not recreated in the reflections below. Slight variations in shade serve to suggest the different planes and depths of colour. As in Plate 32 (page 60) the reflection is a subtle interpretation of its original – trying to include too much detail will only confuse the image.
Detail shown: 11.5 x 9.5cm (4½ x 3¾in)

PLATE 62 (far right) ▷
The rusty orange underside of the hovea leaves gives an added dimension of colour to this design. Given the startling, though simple, butterfly wing pattern and the regular, symmetrical pea flowers, this is a useful device. You may have introduced an element of fantasy, as in Plate 57, but try not to pick insects and flowers which are naturally anathema to each other! Look out for features which will give an added element of interest, such as a variation in the colourway. Similarly a balancing, though inverted geometric – in this case the V-shaped grasses echoing the swallowtail of the butterfly – will give a lively dynamic to the overall study.
14 x 20.25cm (5½ x 8in)

The rolling breakers of the bay echo the smooth curves of the mountains above. Worked in elongated, narrowing bands of seed stitches, they present a contrast in texture to the smooth horizontal stitching of the waters between (see Fig 58). In the immediate foreground the rocks are worked in perpendicular straight stitching, with sharp angles shadow lined. Added interest is created by random details such as the broken fronds of sea kelp and the star fish.

Rocky outcrops, whether on beaches or mountain sides are difficult habitats in which to sustain life. With little soil to nourish root systems, and often low rainfall, plants adapt to retain all the water they can – coarse, leathery leaves hoard whatever precipitation falls and the plants often conserve their energy by flowering rarely, with sometimes less than spectacular effect. An exception is the violet pea (*Hovea longifolia*) an inhabitant of Australasia and a relative of the *acacia* (Plate 62). The Australian Blue Mountain swallowtail (*Papilio Ulysses*) also known as the blue emperor, is fascinated by blue or violet (even artificial objects can stimulate its

Fig 58 ▷
A simple trick like changing texture from long straight stitching to seed stitches in contrasting shades gives the impression of movement in water. As breakers roll in, the white 'sea-horses' rear upwards, breaking into foam: behind them the rising of the waves is shown in dark blue – the water creating its own shadow.

curiosity) and males flock to favourite plants awaiting mates. Presumably this habit of lying in wait and ambushing unwary fellows gave the butterfly its Latin name – Ulysses is credited by Virgil as being the brains behind the ploy of the wooden horse by which Troy was ultimately taken. The Blue Mountain swallowtail has been called the world's most beautiful butterfly: certainly coupled with its size – up to 14cm (5½in) across – it is one of the most impressive.

The iridescent inner areas of the wings should be worked first – smooth fields of radial *opus plumarium* falling back towards the insect's body – leaving voids between the fields where the veining occurs. The deep, black margins of both upper and lower wings are worked next, strata blending smoothly into the peacock-blue interior. Voided lines are then filled by black veins, stem stitched where the teardrop-shaped inner fields of wings are described and where the veins arc, and straight stitched on the lower wings where the veins follow roughly the direction of the radial work. Although only bi-coloured, with a deep blue-black body, the vibrancy of this beautiful butterfly can rival any complex, multi-shaded species. As so often seems to be the case in design, the rule of 'less fuss, more flair' certainly applies to this specimen.

THE TREE LINE

High-rise living is not confined to the dizzy heights of mountain ranges – to a small animal, the top of a tall Scots pine must seem an awe-inspiring location. Those of us who are fortunate enough to live in climates which support large trees can often take them for granted, however, and as a subject for embroidery they present certain challenges until we begin to analyze how the upper reaches of a large tree 'works'. In the same way as becoming familiar with the way in which a flower is constructed makes the interpretation of the subject easier, so, if we understand the basics of tree growth, we can create a more successful portrait.

In Plate 10 (page 15), the dominant feature of the landscape is a large 'stag-headed' oak (*Quercus robur*). The age of the tree has meant that some of its upper boughs have lost their supply of sap and died back, leaving bare, woody 'antlers' above the lush foliage below. A detail of this picture is shown in Plate 63. The key to working any tree realistically is to give it as much detail as possible – once the trunk and larger branches have been worked (with the appropriate shadow lining) smaller branches and then twigs should be created in straight stitching. A bare, winter tree outline is shown in Plate 77, page 125 (see also Fig 59). Once this framework is complete, the tree can be clothed with foliage to transform it into a spring, summer or autumn portrait, depending on the subject of the picture. Plate 63 shows this clothing process in detail. Above and below each twig, seed stitches are applied at an angle to the straight stitching to create leaves – lighter and darker shades used respectively to enhance the ever-present use of light and shade to capture a sense

▽ *Fig 59*

The magnificent English oak is king of the trees – huge boughs rise out of a vast central trunk: as the tree ages its core often becomes rotten and hollow (suggested here by the heavy shadow at its centre) but it still thrives, the thickness of the outer layers of wood sufficient to let vital sap through to the upper branches. Ancient trees become 'stag-headed', bare antlers rising above the leafy canopy in summer. These branches are still easy to spot on the unclothed tree: lacking tiny twigs on which to sport leaves, only the thicker ones remain, as at the centre top of this tree. Working a successful tree in landscape embroidery repays the amount of effort you put in to it! Lots of twigs, therefore lots of tiny leaves, equals realistic effect!

◁ *PLATE 63 (detail of Plate 10)*
The landscape behind the tree is flooded in and
around the branches and leaves keeping the
distant element on a horizontal plane.
Allowing a certain amount of the background
fabric to form a 'halo' around the closer
features, gives an impression of space between
the two. This device is also used on the very
distant trees: the perpendicular groups of
straight stitching which form each individual
clump of foliage are separated by a voided line.
Detail shown: 11.5 x 14cm (4½ x 5½in)

▽ *Fig 60*
The profile of the Douglas fir does not change
from winter to summer. In close-up (Plate 65)
each twig is almost a miniature version of the
main branches with regard to overall shape:
from a central point the twigs/branches pivot
outward along a roughly horizontal line.

of reality. 'Light and dark' can be replaced with 'bright and dull' depending on the species of tree – in Plate 63 the upper leaves are a true green, the lower a rather baser colour, typical of the oak once high summer and harvest time has arrived. At the extreme top left-hand corner of the detail an area of the bare antler is shown. This naked skeleton illustrates how the straight stitched twigs overlie each other – when clothed the leaves follow the same pattern, gradually building up a natural three-dimensional effect.

Exactly the same principles are applied when the subject is worked in miniature. Plate 64 shows a London plane tree (*Platanus x hispanica*) in a typical town park setting. John Tradescant (1608–62), gardener royal to Charles I, is credited with breeding the first London plane, a hybrid of the American and Oriental planes, and many specimens well over 200 years old are still growing vigorously today. One of the few trees which could survive in the soot-laden atmosphere of industrial cities before the passing in the United Kingdom of the Clean Air Act in 1958, the London plane is a haven for small animals and birds in the urban jungle of many inner city locations.

In this miniature, the skeleton of the tree has been worked in a slightly finer gauge than on a full-sized portrait, but the majority of the leaves, although to scale with the rest of the picture, are in a thicker thread. This helps to build up the thickness of the canopy, so that the layering of the foliage gives a convincing depth to the subject. A little of the background fabric is still allowed to show through in places (look at any tree and you will see there is light and air penetrating even the most dense areas of leafing) to suggest a movement in the breeze. This small picture, like the landscape in Plate 10 was a commissioned embroidery – the trees each had personal significance for the people who now own the works. Being able to capture the 'character' of an individual tree is a rewarding experience for any artist.

Conifers present slightly different challenges: as landscape features they are relatively simple (see Fig 60), but in close-up flat pine needles require special consideration. In Plate 65 a firecrest (*Regulus ignicapillus*) – a close relative of the goldcrest, see Plate 25, page 45 – takes up residence in the upper reaches of a Douglas fir (*Pseudotsuga menziesii*). After the redwoods, the Douglas fir is the tallest tree growing on the North American west coast. Introduced into Europe in the first

PLATE 64 ▷
Mounted in a brass fob-topped miniature frame, this embroidery is created by a sequence of (roughly) circular devices – the canopy of the tree, the overall perimeter of the design and the frame itself. Within this theme, the various elements are worked as they would be in a full-sized study – horizontal straight stitching to form the landscape features, a miniaturization of the flowers, and a suggestion of movement by the addition of the flying birds. Remember that even on a very small piece of work it is important to find room for your signature – in years to come it may be of equal interest as the embroidery itself!
6.5cm (2½in) diameter, including frame

◁ *PLATE 65*
*In winter, firecrests may gather with goldcrests
and other small birds, including tits,
conserving their body heat in communal roosts.
This tiny bird can be most easily identified by
its striking black eye stripe. Where black
markings on a bird or butterfly abut a black
background fabric (as here), it can be tempting
to leave the area blank – as with voiding
techniques. However, if the field to be filled is
any larger than a single line, it is important to
work black on black – the texture of your
stitching will be sufficiently different to the
background material to make the embroidery
evident and, if omitted, the break in stitching
will distract the eye from the overall flow of the
design. Work in a good light, make sure your
transferred outline is distinct and you should
have no problems.*
9.5 x 7.5cm (3¾ x 3in)

quarter of the nineteenth century, the newcomer was widely planted as a decorative specimen – and found particular favour in the private forests around Scottish mansions. Later it became a valuable commercial crop and now it is an important timber tree in Britain. The needles of the Douglas fir are long and soft, with an irregular tip. Worked on black, shadow lining is unnecessary, but each needle should be carefully separated from its neighbours, and from the growth twig, by voiding. The chevron stitches of the yew in Plate 25 are replaced by sharply angled lozenges – sliver-slim wedges – of radial *opus plumarium*.

The male flowers of the Douglas fir are shaped like tiny, golden fir cones: in Plate 65 they are worked in seed stitches, the colour graduating from yellow to amber. Mature fir cones usually begin life upright and then turn over to hang downwards and allow the seeds to fall out. Once the seed of the Douglas fir has set, it produces a young willowy tree, rather prone, on light soils, to be blown down. Having survived its difficult early years, however, the tree grows tall and straight, its heavy, durable timber excellent for building work, fine veneers and high-quality plywood. In North America it is called the Oregon pine. Early settlers who took the Oregon Trail in their covered wagons, may well have made it one of the traditional motifs in their appliquéd quilting – it certainly bears a striking resemblance to some early designs.

CHAPTER SEVEN

XANADU

*The night was dominated by degrees of smallness
In the substances beneath their feet and hands –
Boulders or pea gravel or flaked rock
Or pea sand or sand itself or grit or dust or gossamer.*

Frank Herbert
Dune

OUT OF THIS WORLD

PLATE 67 ▷

The flowers of Lothlórien – Tolkein's Elven realm of Middle-earth. In Anglo-Saxon tradition St John's wort was a herb of protection against witchcraft and 'elf-shot', whilst the nodding head of the fritillary lily afforded it a tradition similar to that of the exotic imperial lily (Plate 35, page 64). The chequer-work pattern on the bell of the lily is worked in fine laddering (similar to the cathedral tower in Plate 53), white radial work falling back to the core of the flower, and needlewoven through with a pale green at right angles. This colourway is reversed to create the 'negative' shading on the underside of the petals, giving a predominantly green effect.

9 x 9.5cm (3½ x 3¾in)

◁ *PLATE 66*

'Planet Earth is blue. . .' David Bowie's Space Oddity *captured an astronaut's awe on seeing his planet from space. Constructed from two images taken during the Apollo 17 lunar flight (7–19 December 1972) this composite study captures the majesty of a view very few of us will ever see in real life. The 384,000km (240,000 mile) gulf between Earth and the moon took the Apollo astronauts about sixty-six hours to traverse. On Christmas Eve 1968 Apollo 8 circled the moon, taking mankind for the first time out of sight of his own planet. On seeing Earth again, crew member Bill Anders recalled, 'It's very delicate. . . It reminded me of a Christmas tree ornament'. I can see the likeness. . . a blown glass ball of many colours. By working the Earth in floss silk, a sheen is achieved despite the fracturing effect of the split stitch. This produces a very effective variation in shades, in contrast to the universally straight stitching of the lunar landscape. When hung this picture should be lit from the top left – from the Earthrise!*

Embroidery shown life-size:

44.5 x 28cm (17½in x 11in)

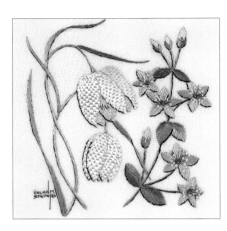

Embroidery has always afforded the imaginative mind an avenue of escape from the mundane. In past centuries when it was often a woman's lot to be restricted to the world of home and hearth, the planning, design and execution of her embroideries was one of the few areas of her existence where she could be free – to explore, to interpret, to fantasize. The physical restrictions of a life in captivity could be forgotten in the planning of new projects – for over fifteen years of captivity Mary Queen of Scots lived vicariously through her embroideries – and their final realization.

As we enter the third millennium many concepts which once seemed only fantastic flights of fancy have become reality. We can travel the globe at the speed of sound, live in biospheres of our own choosing (making the deserts bloom and the rain forests habitable) and, soon perhaps, visit worlds other than our own. Already 'space tourists' can view our planet from the relative safety of a man-made satellite and our generation has seen 'Earthrise' from the surface of the moon.

Plate 66 is a picture that I have wanted to create for years. . . Is it mad to try and capture the whole world in embroidery? The swirling white and blue masses of water and cloud, the hot red deserts of the great African continent, the distinctive outlines of the Arabian Gulf and the Nile basin, the cradles of our civilization, and the light of the world, the reflections of our life-giving sun illuminating the barren stretches of the lunar landscape – all this can be caught in its diversity, in materials as ancient as spun silk and as modern as stripped cellophane.

Just as we have become familiar with the waxing and waning of the moon, so, from space, the Earth appears as a crescent, a half-Earth and a full-Earth as it orbits the sun. In December 1972 the Apollo 17 astronauts were the first to see a full-Earth as they began their lunar journey. The African rain forests are hidden by clouds but the Sahara Desert to the north and Kalahari to the south are clear – so is the island of Madagascar. It is late spring in the southern hemisphere and the Antarctic ice-cap is at its brightest, partly hidden by the Sculptured Hills on the moon's horizon. Apollo 17's lunar module, *Challenger*, landed in the Taurus-Littrow Valley in the shadow of Bear Mountain, the North and South Massifs rising over 2,150m (7,000ft) above Camelot Crater to the right of the picture. The stark lunar landscape is devoid of colour save for the reflected nuances of the Earth, but the rock-strewn, black-shadowed plateaux have a grandeur all their own.

I have embroidered the Earth entirely in split stitch, beginning at the outer periphery and spiralling inwards, working in narrow bands of stitching to maintain an even flow and, consequently, changing colour often. The swirling weather systems flow one into the next, each element of the planet's climate influenced by its neighbour, only the anti-cyclone in the southern Indian Ocean apparently forming itself into a threatening mass of conflicting winds and air pressures. By contrast, the lunar surface is worked in straight stitching throughout, horizontal for the flat, dusty planes and dunes, vertical for the boulders and rocky outcrops. There is little subtle variation in the monochrome – the faces of the rocks which catch the light are brash, the shadowed aspects so deeply shaded as to be black against black. Even so, I have stitched this deepest shade, rather than leaving it blank – a change in texture catches the eye sufficiently to suggest perspective and depth (Fig 62).

Movement? Apart from the majesty of the Earthrise itself, only the moon-walker disturbs the tranquillity of the scene, his long shadow cast by the light of his home planet, his footprints in the lunar dust destined to remain undisturbed for aeons, for there is no wind on the moon.

Unchanging too are the worlds created by great imaginations – Tolkein's Middle-earth, Lewis's Narnia, Peake's Gormenghast, Herbert's Dune: alternate universes in which the laws of our own world cease to exist, either through the evolution of an entirely altered reality or from the unfathomable logic of a civilization wholly alien to our own. But however fertile an imagination may be, it must to some extent draw upon its own experience and observation to bring a new world into being. In *The Lord of the Rings*, Tolkein described the land of Lothlórien, home of the Elves '. . .all about the green hillsides the grass was studded with small golden flowers shaped like stars. Among them, nodding on slender stalks, were other flowers, white and the palest green: they glimmered as a mist among the rich hue of the grass.'

It is not difficult to identify the flowers which inspired this reverie: the star-like golden flowers are a perfect description of perforate St John's wort (*Hypericum perforatum*) and the nodding white and green bells are the rare pale form of the snake's-head lily (*Fritillaria meleagris*) (Plate 67). Tolkein was a professor of Anglo-Saxon literature and would have known that both these flowers were steeped in magical associations – like much of the imagery and mythology of his Middle-earth, the Elven flowers of *elanor* and *niphredil* were drawn from the traditions of his own world.

Even more extraordinary is the fertile imagination which created Mervyn Peake's strange and macabre land of Gormenghast. His thousand-page trilogy is set in a world of 'dusk and sharpness like a needle in velvet', a universe where logic is less important than tradition, where the Countess Gertrude's hundred snow-white cats interweave with each other 'like a living arabesque'. How can one fail to be inspired by such descriptions? In Plate 68, one of the Countess' cats reclines on its velvet cushion, a textured halo of swirling light forming an aura of colour around it.

Like the planet Earth in Plate 66 the white cat is worked in split stitch – here in a single strand of fine white silk, shaded with grey and silver. Perspective has been deliberately altered to add to the other-worldliness of the subject – the cat appears to hover weightless above the cushion as though the velvet were simply a manifestation of its own sense of comfort. Blending filaments are couched in a

▽ *Fig 61*

Leaving the planet does not mean leaving behind the rules of light and shade. With no atmosphere to soften the reflected light of the sun, shadows on the moon are even more stark than usual. With light from above, stitches can be angled to create an accentuated effect, dark shadows becoming inkier as they reach ground level and extend. See also Fig 5, page 17.

▽ *Fig 62*

The Camelot Crater is just one of millions which scatter the moon's surface. Again, light and shade create the desired effect.
Top: Two rough ellipses form the mouth and base of the crater.
Middle: Horizontal stitches suggest the floor, whilst other straight stitches angle inward toward it.
Bottom: Deep shadows toward the light source indicate that this is a concave rather than convex feature.

· · · · · · · · ·

meandering, random pattern around the main subject, opalescent seed beads forming a circle of deeper texture at the periphery of the design.

My own tabby and white cat, Ragnar, often proves the perfect model, equally at ease amid foliage or fabric (Fig 63). A few elementary squiggles or sweeps suggest the appropriate settings. If you aim for a realistic study, try to make the background relatively simple – for a feline fantasy, however, you can be as far-fetched as you chose.

Fig 63 △
Cats are notoriously difficult subjects, but at ease they are natural models! The striping on a tabby cat gives a good indication of the line to be followed by your directional stitching.

PLATE 68 ▷
'Deep, unhurried purring. . . like the voice of an ocean in the throat of a shell.' Mervyn Peake's description of the Countess' cats rings true for every cat lover. A cat at rest is, to say the least, a relaxed subject. Remember if you sketch a cat from life to translate into embroidery (Fig 63) you need not include every detail of fur and whisker. . . a suggestion of the sweep of the coat to guide your subsequent stitches and perhaps an aide-mémoire to remind you later of the object of the model's attention (if any!) will be a useful addition. Here, white whiskers are worked against the background of the piece, but black against the white fur of the cat itself. Minute details such as this lend a sense of reality to even the most abstract arrangement.
14 x 14cm (5½ x 5½in)

· · · · · · · · ·

INNER SPACE

The world of Faerie is one which has hovered on the edge of man's imagination since time immemorial. It is the 'perilous realm' reached by the Golden Thread of many mythologies (see *The Myth and Magic of Embroidery*); a world where the normal rules of existence cease to operate, where the inhabitants may be large or small, seen or unseen as the spirit moves them, where the concepts of good and evil are largely irrelevant.

The 'fairy tale' interpretation of this strange land is inhabited by the tiny, lithe sprites and pixies of children's story books: fragile little beings of field and meadow, the Tom Thumbs and Thumbelinas of Disney's magic animation. Any little girl (and many big ones!) would love a study such as this, the Sapphire Fairy (Plate 69). The L-shaped arrangement of the flowers, the choice of forget-me-nots – the flower of lasting affection – the banded damselfly wings of the fairy herself, all make this a design intended to convey love, light and harmony.

Like the 'cocktail lady' in Plate 50 (page 86) the flesh tones and texture of this study have been worked in a minute speckling stitch. Fine shadow lining has been used to define the lower outlines of limbs, etc., and the face picked out in a similarly fine back thread – eyes nose and mouth all suggested by sketching in straight stitches before the working of the speckling. A wild mane of hair is suggested by lowlights in fine black, interspersed with golden threads, worked zigzag fashion from crown to tip. Very fine, long, radial stitches describe the wings, the 'band' created by interspersing blue-green threads between the black structural stitches to form a gibbous moon motif.

The tiny ethereal fairies of nursery books are a fairly late invention – the longer established residents of Faerie are the 'old Gods' of Celtic and Norse mythology: Bran and Branwen, Wayland Smith and the Lady of the Lake – and her sister Mab, Queen of the Faeries (Plate 70). 'Queen' in this instance means not just sovereign but the embodiment of the female (Old English '*cwen*') and midwife to the Faerie realm. She also 'delivered' men of their dreams – when Shakespeare's Romeo says, 'I dreamed a dream last night', Mercutio replies, 'O, then, I see Queen Mab hath been with you'. I have shown her on a watered silk of lilac, mauve and green and wearing the traditional gown of the aristocratic lady of Faerie – 'grass green silk and velvet fine' (Thomas the Rhymour, trad.). Again, there are parallels with Plate 50 – the flesh is worked similarly and here the gown is also worked, shadow lined and highlighted, to recreate long folds of fabric. The shift and petticoat is in gold-coloured silk with metallic thread studding – a real amethyst and feather represent dreams taking flight.

There are occasions when a startling backdrop serves to enhance an embroidery – here the hand-dyed silk suggests the colours of the 'crystal caves' of legend, home of Merlin the magician and also the earth-bound domain of Mab. On a patterned backdrop it is important to position the main motif carefully – the face is located over a pale area of fabric, allowing the speckling stitch to be worked without hindrance, and distinct striations of colour have been aligned with various

PLATE 69 ▷

The Sapphire Fairy is a fantasy of blue and green. Tiny, uncut Iolite and sodalite stones edge the pool, whilst the pink buds and blue flowers of the forget-me-not define the corners of the study.

11.5 x 14.5cm (4¹⁄₂ x 5³⁄₄in)

▽ *Fig 64*

On complex drapery it is important to establish the outer and inner surfaces of the fabric. Shown here without subtle shadowing it is easy to see which side is visible through the folds.

elements of the figure at waist and shoulder height. Below, irregular shapes suggest boulders and rock formations. The merest suggestion of an embroidered setting has been included in the shape of a green foothold and impressionistic flowers. An elliptical halo of rainbow-coloured blending filaments radiates from the figure – these fall back to an invisible 'core' in the shape of the amethyst.

Speckling stitch can also be used to describe larger fields of colour in greater detail, shadows created gradually by interspersing deeper shades of blush and greys into the flesh tones (Plate 71). Here, a nymph-like figure is on the verge of maturity, a transformation as wonderful as the metamorphosis of the butterfly from chrysalis to adulthood. The colour themes in Plate 70 have been recreated in this study but to very different effect. Working on a plain, pale background, a naturalistic setting has been created in the shape of the common mallow (*Malva sylvestris*) which forms the framing feature for the study. We look 'through' this element to the action

◁ *PLATE 70*
'Arise up, Miss, all in your gown of green,
You are as fine a lady as wait upon the Queen'.
The ancient Cornish Padstow May song calls
upon the power of the colour of the Faeries –
green – to give the village girls status. Many
old country customs forbade the wearing of
green at certain Christian festivals as it held
too many connotations of a pagan past.
14 x 9cm (5¹⁄₂ x 3¹⁄₂in)

▽ *PLATE 72 (Detail of Plate 71 overleaf)*
A distinct transfer line is a huge help when
creating a detailed embroidery. Don't be
tempted to rush over the preparation of your
work, even impressionistic techniques benefit
from an outline which defines specific contours.
Detail shown (figure height): 12.75cm (5in)

beyond, the foreground features repeated in miniature in scale with the figure – mallows and butterflies hold the girl's attention. An implication of height is introduced by working a suggestion of sky at a low level behind the figure – immediately we feel ourselves to be elevated, on a hilltop location parallel with the flush of dawn on the skyline.

The gradual build-up of the speckling stitches is seen in greater detail in Plate 72. As ever, the shadow line is worked first, only then the chosen filling technique is allowed to bring life to the figure. Beginning with the areas of deepest shade, a dark grey is worked along the contours of the shadow line, blending into a paler grey before beginning the application of the first flesh tones. The dimpled knee, the elbow and the calf muscle are similarly defined, together with fine details such as the tiny toe-nails and delicate facial features. As work continues, the inner fields fill up to create the various convex and concave curves of the body. From a high crown

on the top of her head, short directional stitches suggesting the girl's hair are carefully and gradually worked in.

In Scandinavian mythology the 'hill people' were a race apart – something between elves and humans, who dwelt beneath small tors and barrows. A traditional way of entering the underworld was to walk seven (some say nine or even thirteen) times around certain hills, whereupon a door would miraculously open in the hillside, allowing access to the Faerie realm. During the Middle Ages, children who mysteriously disappeared were often thought to have been spirited away into this strange other dimension. There are some instances too of the roles being reversed – at the turn of the thirteenth century two 'green children' were found wandering near the village of Woolpit in Suffolk, England. Adopted by the villagers, they gradually learnt to speak English (their language was quite unintelligible when found) and said they came from a green hill called 'St Martin's Land'. Such 'changelings' appear quite often in folklore. As our world now enters the New Age of Aquarius a re-kindled belief in such tales is emerging. Certainly they are inspirational.

THE LAST UNICORN

At the flick of a switch technology now allows us to create stunning laser shows and holographic images. A computer keyboard animates three-dimensional beings on our VDU – we can interact with 'virtual' pets, people, aliens and chimeras. Through the Internet we can communicate instantly with friends on the other side of the world and 'urban myths' disseminate at lightning speed through chat-rooms and websites. Is there anywhere left in our hectic, high-tech lives for wonder?

Oh, yes. When a young child suddenly becomes aware of Christmas, sees their first Santa Claus, hears a fairy story for the first time, picks up a crayon and realizes that there is such a thing as creativity, then the wonder of the human spirit comes to the surface. The natural world constantly challenges the artist: a scattering of ephemera on a spider's web (Plate 4), the tiny, fragile sea-horse (Plate 15), the wide-eyed beauty of the fennec fox (Plate 31) and the startling colours of humming-birds (Plates 1, 41 and 42). Sweeping landscapes can take the breath away, from the intimate rolling fields and meadows of the Old World (Plate 10) to the startling contrasts of the New (Plates 29 and 60). Every time I am presented with a new idea, fresh inspiration, a seemingly impossible subject, I wonder at the apparently infinite ability of needle and thread to rise to the moment.

Plate 73 was one of those (in this case man-made!) challenges – the 'Horse of the Year Show' in London: three prancing Connemara ponies, trappings, harness and Father Christmas on his sleigh laden with gifts – not a figment of the imagination, but an actual event to be captured in silk! Where to begin and where to end? This was a specific commission and Santa had to appear to be emerging from a 'tunnel' – actually the prop-room's finest cardboard and fibre-glass creation!

The arrangement of the ponies, one leader and two harnessed together at the rear is called a 'unicorn', and like the unicorns of legend, this was a hard subject to capture. It had to be treated impressionistically – confines of scale dictated this – but

△ *Fig 65*

Throughout this book we have explored light and shade. This horse's head could simply be etched and dashed in black to give a 'pen and ink' effect.

△ *PLATE 73*
Merry Christmas!
16 x 10cm (6½ x 4in)

also in enough detail to satisfy the eye of a expert horseman. The ponies themselves were sketched from photographs of the event with the harness and tack in situ (see Fig 65). Embroidered in pure white silk, shadowed by greys, much the same principle of contouring (this time in directional work) was used as in Plate 72. Father Christmas himself and his wild jumble of presents is really just a mass of brightly coloured geometrics, shadowed and stitched accordingly, movement

PLATE 74 (Detail of Plate 2) ▷
The unicorn looks back to the ancient West,
traditionally the route toward the 'Other
World'. The palest silver-grey is the only shade
used to shadow this ethereal being, other than
this and pure white silk, only the unicorn's
spiral horn is worked in fine silver metallic
thread, whipped in black.
Detail shown: 15.25 x 10.75cm (6 x 4¼in)

suggested by the hoof-prints of the pounding horseshoes and the flicking of Santa's switch. They might not be magic reindeer, but these ponies are definitely 'flying' – from a world of reality into one of make-believe.

My world of embroidery is one of limitless possibilities. Never believe that a project is too complex, a concept too outlandish, an idea too far-fetched but remember that true embroidery is an art with a long and noble history and that however avante-garde an invention may be its interpretation should remain based upon a drawing of thread through fabric, the interplay of stitches following certain conventions. A prancing horse can be rendered convincingly by sweeping stitches to the contours of its body – why, then, should the addition of wings be a problem? Elegant, extended wings are a joy in radial and directional *opus plumarium*, primary and secondary feathers overlapping to catch the upflow of air as they beat – should it faze us if they belong to a unicorn rather than a bird? (see Plate 74). A landscape should support and give substance to a subject – why should not solid ground be substituted by a shimmering swirl of gossamer, unspun silk? Allow your imagination to soar with the unicorn.

▽ *PLATE 75*
A giant sagebrush (Plurophyllum speciosum) *seems an unlikely inhabitant of the Antarctic, but even at the very edge of the world nature's superlative palette of colour can offer inspiration. At the centre of each daisy-like flower is a pincushion of brown velvet, apparently studded with minute needles.*
7.5 x 10.75cm (3 x 4½in)

AFTERWORD

Far to the South, less than a thousand miles from the Antarctic circle, on the distant Antipodean islands, tall spikes of wormwood and sagebrush, giant forget-me-nots and delicate primula warm the cold landscape. In the brief summer they burst into colour, reflected perhaps in the towering bulk of passing icebergs – for they bloom within the equatorial limit of these ocean giants.

The story goes that Brithelm searches the skies from the North Star to the Southern Cross. So far he has not found his love, but he still hangs out the great embroidery to comfort his soul and remind him of all that he has lost. The curtain of the Aurora Australis hangs in the cold night sky. . .

BASIC TECHNIQUES

PLATE 76 ▷
These techniques, including the use of simple radial stitching, opus plumarium and dalmatian dog, are all fully explored in The Embroiderer's Countryside Embroidery *shown life-size:*
20.5 x 28cm (8 x 11in)

The techniques explored here are fully explained in the 'Stitch Variations' section included in the Masterclass sections of *Helen M. Stevens' Embroidered Flowers* and *Embroidered Butterflies* (see Select Bibliography for details, page 142).

Plates 76 and 77 are composite designs in the form of samplers which illustrate many of the techniques mentioned below. Where appropriate, the individual motifs are reproduced as line drawings to simplify the notes.

SHADOW LINING AND VOIDING

These two techniques define and differentiate between planes of stitching.

Shadow lining – Only used in work on a pale background. Imagine where the light source originates within your picture and work a fine black line of stitching along the opposite edge of each motif (see Fig A1).

Voiding – Used in work on a pale or dark background. Where one element of

a design overlaps another, leave a narrow line void of stitching. The line should be approximately the width of the gauge of thread used.

Subdued voiding – Used to soften outlines where a less definite demarcation zone between fields is required, especially on animals and birds. Choose a colour which matches the upper plane and, at exactly the same angle, work straight stitches in a fine thread spanning the voiding line (see squirrel in Plate 76).

OPUS PLUMARIUM

This literally means 'feather work' and imitates the way in which a bird's feathers lie on its body – smoothly, but with an infinite capacity to change direction. The angle of the stitches sweeps around without breaking the flow of the stitching. This catches the light, giving a three-dimensional effect.

Radial opus plumarium – Close ranks

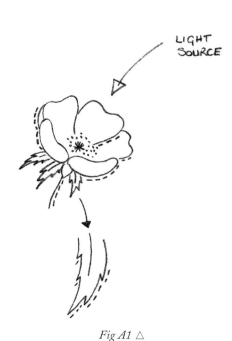

LIGHT SOURCE

Fig A1 △
The imagined light source within the picture is coming from the top right-hand corner. All elements opposite to the light source should be shadow lined, as indicated by the hatched line

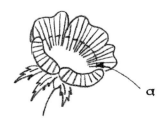

a

Fig A2 △
Radial lines shown suggest only about one in four of the stitches needed to work the motif. Hatched line 'a' shows the approximate point at which the second stratum of stitching should begin

Fig A3 △
Opposite angle embroidery is used where a leaf or other motif reflexes. Note the angle of stitches on one surface of the motif and exactly reverse it for the other side

HELEN
STEVENS

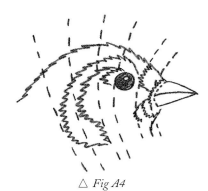

△ Fig A4

Opus plumarium is so called because it imitates the way in which a bird's feathers lie on its body. Here, radial strata roughly equate to the markings on the bird's head – the eye should always be worked at an opposite angle to the main field of the embroidery

Fig A5 ▽

The darker hatching (1) indicates the inner core of the work. The surrounding wedges of radial work (2) are worked smoothly into the core. Open arrows indicate the direction in which individual stitches should be taken. The hatched arrow is a reminder that the whole motif should sweep outwards from the body of the animal

of stitching apparently emanating from the same core and describing a wedge, arc or full circle. Stitches are taken from the outside edge of the motif inwards, where necessary disappearing behind their neighbours to advance the angle of stitching. Two or more strata of stitching my be necessary to build up a broad motif (see Fig A2 and Fig A4).

Directional opus plumarium – Where the core of a motif is elongated (such as in the central vein of a simple leaf) the stitches should flow smoothly along its length (see Fig A3). Again, always stitch inwards.

Opposite angle embroidery – Used where a motif reflexes, eg, on a leaf or petal. The reverse of the subject should be worked at the same, but opposite, angle to the existing *opus plumarium* (see Fig A3).

DALMATIAN DOG TECHNIQUE

The method of incorporating features within *opus plumarium* to form a single smooth plane: ie, work black spots and then embroider a white dog around them. Ensure that the elements to be included are worked at the same angle of stitching as the embroidery which is to surround them. Blend together smoothly without outline or voiding (see butterfly in Plate 77).

STRAIGHT STITCH

Any technique which involves the use of either (1) single straight stitches to represent a whole motif, eg, a single blade of grass, or (2) straight stitches worked in unison, but without imitating *opus plumarium*; eg, horizontally to represent grassland, water, sky, etc, or in the perpendicular for tree trunks, etc.

STEM STITCH

Always work from the tip of any line to be described and *with* the curve of the subject. Bring your needle out just to the outside of the curve and put it in just on the inside of the curve. The line may be made fine or broad depending upon how much the stitches are allowed to overlap, or may graduate by increasing the overlap along the length of the curve. Similarly to illustrate a coil, work small stitches to describe the tight curve at its centre and gradually lengthen the stitches as the curve becomes gentler. To reflex the curve, take one stitch through its predecessor, directly along the pattern line, at the point where the curve changes direction, subsequently bringing the needle up on the 'new' outside of the curve.

RIVER STITCH

Method of working *opus plumarium* when the field to be covered sweeps from one direction to another, such as on a squirrel's tail. Work a core of embroidery as a narrow band of *opus plumarium* and on either side work fan-shaped wedges of radial stitching, increasing and decreasing the angle of the wedge as necessary to describe the curve (see Fig A5).

SNAKE STITCH

This stitch is used to describe long, sinuous shapes.

Simple snake stitch – Begin at the tip of the motif, taking the first stitch in the direction of the curve to be described. For subsequent stitches, bring the needle out on the outside of the curve and in on the inside. Work smoothly down the motif.

Reflexing snake stitch – Begin at the point of reflex, where the direction of the curve changes, and work first toward one extremity and then the other (see Fig A6).

Fig A6 △
Snake stitch. One direction is always from the centre to the tip of a motif, the other from the centre to the core end

TICKING

Short stitches overlaying *opus plumarium* worked at exactly the same angle as the underlying work, but taken in the opposite direction. Often used to describe the fine markings on the heads and underparts of birds.

STUDDING

Short stitches overlaying *opus plumarium* worked at the opposite angle to the underlying stitches. Often used when scale does not permit the use of dalmatian dog technique (see miniature woodpecker in medallion in Plate 77).

SHOOTING STITCH

A long straight stitch taken in the opposite direction to underlying radial work. Used to create subtle streaks on petals, and so on.

LADDERING

This is used to illustrate chequer-board markings. Fill the field to be worked with straight stitching or *opus plumarium*, as appropriate. Using a contrasting shade, weave backwards and forwards through the existing stitches, leaving the work fairly loose so that it can be 'pushed' into the correct position.

SEED STITCH

Worked directly onto the background fabric or occasionally over underlying embroidery, seed stitches are fine, short straight stitches (see centre of rose in Plate 76 and village scene in Plate 77).

CHEVRON STITCH

Used to convey any straight prickle or similar motif. Take two long straight stitches, angled to meet. Infill with a third straight stitch, if necessary. Using a finer thread, take a long straight stitch through the body of the spine, extending beyond the tip, if a particularly sharp tip is required.

HONEYCOMB STITCH

Used for dragonfly's wings, etc. Transfer only the outline of the wing on to the fabric. Work fine radial stitches from the edge of the wing to the body of the insect. Lay a short stitch over two radial stitches at right angles and repeat, brickwork fashion. As these stitches are tightened the radial stitches will gradually be pulled in opposite directions to form a honeycomb pattern. Never shadow line. Overlay with specialist blending filament to create cellular sheen.

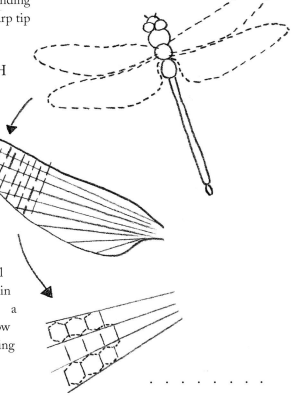

Fig A7 ▽
Honeycomb stitch. The 'brick' stitches must slightly overlap the radial stitches so that when they are tightened, they will gently separate the underlying work to reveal the honeycombing

HELEN
STEVENS

COBWEBBING

Work a framework of outer threads. Add dissecting stitches similar to the spokes of a wheel. Whip around the spokes to suspend the body of the cobweb from the framework without stitching through the background fabric.

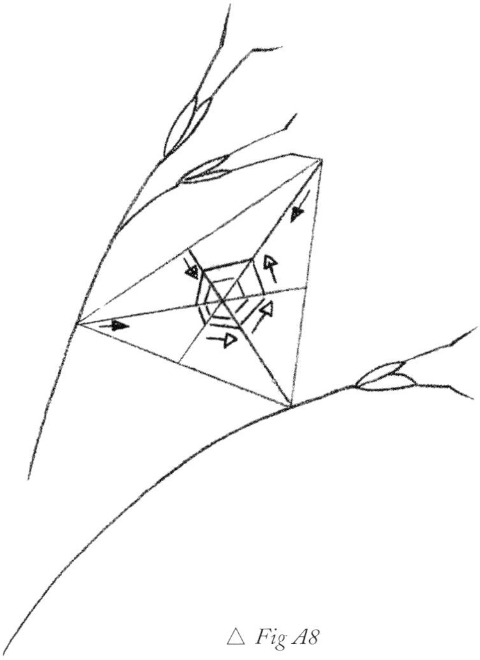

△ *Fig A8*
Cobwebbing. The spokes are formed by three directional stitches as shown by the black arrows. The circular filaments are added, by whipping the spokes: ie, by taking a tiny stitch around and behind each one and stretching the thread between them

FLOATING EMBROIDERY

A technique which allows threads to lie loosely on the background fabric, falling into spontaneous shapes. Do not transfer the design to be formed on to the background fabric. Take a long stitch from the inside to the outside of the motif, putting a finger under the thread to keep it away from the fabric. Take a very small stitch at the outer point to

bring the thread back to the surface. Take a third stitch back to the core of the motif, again keeping a finger beneath the thread. Repeat the process, removing the finger when several strands have built up (see Fig A9).

ETCHING

A method of shadowing used primarily on buildings in landscape work. Worked as a patch of perpendicular straight stitches (usually in black) below an overhanging feature (see village scene in Plate 77).

DOTTING

A technique mainly used for buildings consisting of very short, closely worked stitches arranged randomly and usually in a variety of colours, blending smoothly. Used to create grainy surfaces in close-up, or rough surfaces in the distance. Worked around etching (see village scene in Plate 77).

DASHING

Used to convey smooth surfaces in architectural embroidery, eg, plasterwork, thatches, etc. Worked in long, straight, perpendicular stitches from one field of etching, or other feature, to the next (see village scene in Plate 77).

MINIATURIZING

This is the process of extrapolating the essential features of a large study and translating them into miniature form. Usually, dalmatian dog technique is replaced by studding, and several strata of radial stitching reduced to a single field. The finest of threads are essential (see medallion in Plate 77).

◁ *PLATE 77*
Expanding the close-up techniques explored in Plate 76, together with landscape and other features, this sampler is inspired by work in The Embroiderer's Country Album Embroidery *shown life-size:*
9 x 28.5cm (7¹⁄₂ x 11¹⁄₄in)

▽ *Fig A9*
Small black arrows (1) indicate the outward stitch, a small stitch is taken at the apex, and open arrows (2) show the return of the thread to the core

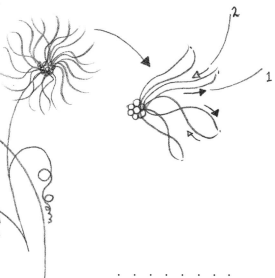

Fig B1 △
With the thumb on the outer ring of the
tambour frame, the fingers of the hand should
just be able to reach the centre of the circle.
Similarly, with a larger frame, with the elbow
at the ring, the fingers should reach the centre

APPENDIX B
THE PRACTICALITIES

WORKING CONDITIONS AND EQUIPMENT

LIGHTING

Daylight is the finest and most natural light of all but if daylight is not available or not sufficient a good spotlight is a worthwhile investment.

Always work with the spotlight in the same position in relation to your embroidery, so that you become familiar with the angle of the light. Any shadow cast by your hand will soon become unnoticeable. Keep the light in such a position that any shadow will not cut across the stitching.

If you are working on a fine fabric, avoid having a high level of light immediately behind the work, as this will have the effect of making the fabric transparent, and can be very distracting. If you are working outdoors keep the sun behind you, but wear a hat or use a sun shade, as concentration plus sunlight can lead to headaches and eyestrain.

EMBROIDERY FRAMES

In fine flat embroidery the tension of the background fabric is all important and it is essential to work on an embroidery frame. Round 'tambour' frames, so called because they resemble a tambourine, are best suited to fine work, as the tension they produce is entirely uniform. A free-standing frame is especially useful when techniques such as couching are to be included in the work, as these require two hands.

Tambour frames are available in a range of materials, but whichever frame is chosen it is essential that it should feel comfortable to use. If the diameter is more than approximately 35cm (14in) it can become too heavy, when dressed, to be hand-held without making the arm tired, so it should therefore be free-standing. Ideally, a hand-held tambour frame should be small enough for the fingers of the hand in which it is held to reach from the outer rim to the centre of the frame without straining, as they will be able to guide the needle when it is on the reverse of the fabric. For free-standing frames, a good rule of thumb is that the embroiderer should be able to reach to the centre of the dressed frame without stretching unduly when the elbow is at the level of the outer rim.

OTHER EQUIPMENT

The choice of smaller tools is a personal one. Embroidery scissors must be small, fine and sharp, whatever their design. The finer your choice of threads, the sharper and keener the scissors must be.

Needles, too, must be chosen with the specific use of threads and fabric in mind. It is a good idea to have a selection of various sizes to avoid frustration when a new piece of work is begun. Sizes 5 to 10 are generally the most useful. For metallic threads use either a wide-eyed embroidery needle or a crewel needle of suitable size, depending on the technique.

If you use a thimble, be sure that it fits snugly and be careful that it has no worn or jagged edged which may catch in the work – this applies to all the tools discussed.

MATERIALS

There are no 'right' or 'wrong' choices when it comes to choosing fabric and thread so long as certain practical considerations are borne in mind. For so-called flat-work embroidery which must be worked in a frame, it is essential that the fabric chosen for the background does not stretch. If it stretches even slightly while embroidery is in progress, when removed from the frame it will contract to its normal size, and the embroidery will be distorted.

Larger pictures should be worked on heavier fabrics, smaller studies on light-weights, but this rule can be adapted to the particular needs of the picture in question.

Try to avoid fabrics with too loose a weave, as too many stitches will be vying for space in too few threads of warp and weft and the result will be unsatisfactory. Pure cotton and linen evenweaves are ideal, but as a general rule for this type of 'freestyle' embroidery, if the weave is open enough to be used for counted thread embroidery it is too wide for us!

The choice of threads depends upon a number of factors. *Stranded cottons*, such as DMC, are adaptable and widely available in a large range of colours. When split down into single threads they can be delicate enough to convey all but the finest details, and are fine enough to allow themselves to be 'mixed' in the needle. Avoid those skeins which vary their shades throughout their length; they are rarely convincing. It is better to re-thread your needle several times with slightly different shades. Shiny rayons and nylons can also be attractive, but their colours may not be as natural as you could wish, so choose carefully.

Pure silk threads are, of course, the finest and most enjoyable to use, though their behaviour in the needle can be frustrating to beginners. There are many different types of silk thread to choose from. 'Floss' silks are untwisted and therefore very shiny. The advantage of using floss is that it can be split down into very fine threads for the minutest detailed work, and then used doubled, or even trebled, to describe the more substantial parts of the design. For this reason it is ideal when it comes to 'mixing' colours in the needle. An almost infinite variety of shades can be achieved, which is particularly important for natural history subjects. The disadvantage of floss is that by virtue of its untwisted state it can fragment in the needle during the course of working, and, especially if you have rough skin, can catch, fray and generally become very irritating! One solution to this problem is to make sure that your hands remain as smooth and soft as possible, and remember that a rough fingernail (or any other jagged edge) can damage your work almost beyond repair if it catches in embroidery already in situ.

Twisted silks are slightly easier to work with and also have a glorious shine. If they are not twisted too tightly, they may be split down into finer strands for detailed work, and then used in their original state for covering large areas. They are also useful in combination with floss silks to describe areas which do not require such a high level of sheen, for instance, buildings, roads and other man-made aspects of country life.

Stranded silks are a fairly recent innovation. These are a great boon to anyone used to stranded cottons, as they are in similar format and may be used either split into single threads or as up

Note: Much of the information contained in Appendix B is explained in greater detail in *The Embroiderer's Countryside*, pages 125–34.

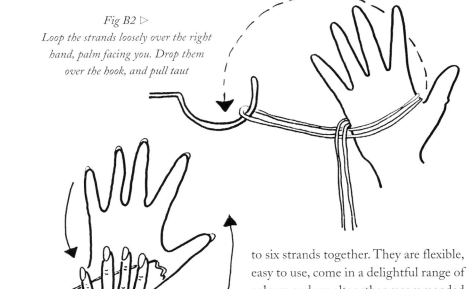

Fig B2 ▷
Loop the strands loosely over the right hand, palm facing you. Drop them over the hook, and pull taut

Fig B3 △
Holding the strand(s) firmly against the heel of the right hand, roll them upwards with the fingertips of the left. Bringing the left hand downwards at the same rate helps to create a smoother thread

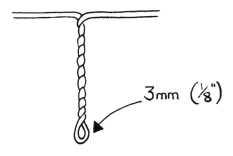

3mm (⅛")

Fig B4 △
Scale x 2 approximately. Releasing the tension allows the thread to twist on to itself. If the correct tension has been achieved it should do so smoothly, form the appropriate loop and disentangle itself easily when pulled straight

to six strands together. They are flexible, easy to use, come in a delightful range of colours and are altogether recommended as having the best elements of both floss and twisted silk.

Initially you will need to buy a range of universally useful colours which will adapt themselves to your preferred subject matter. Decide upon about six basics and get up to three shades of each. For instance, green is obviously a prerequisite of any countryside embroidery project, so buy a true mid-toned green, together with a paler version of the same colour and a darker one for shadowing, etc. Similarly with browns, pinks, blues, yellow-orange and lilac. Needless to say, white and black are also essentials.

The choice of *metallic thread* is wide and varied; plan an excursion to a good needlework shop and have fun choosing for yourself!

Finally, of course, there are all the little extras which make collecting threads and materials more than a practical job and take it into the realms of fantasy. Specialist threads, tiny seed pearls and beads, and the occasional sequin and feather all deserve a place in some secret little glory-hole at the back of your workbox.

TWISTING FLOSS SILK

As you become more advanced in your designs you may find that you wish to mix several types of thread in a single picture – for instance a pure silk embroidery may need to incorporate a number of different textures in the same colours. Silk is expensive but it is possible to effectively double your range of colours by learning the simple technique of plying or twisting, thus creating a finished silk thread with a matt lustre rather than a high gloss.

When using several strands of silk together in the needle to create a single thread (such as when mixing colours), the single thread created is referred to as being *two into one* (written 2/1) or *three into one* (3/1) and so on depending upon how many strands are being used. This may be followed by 'F' or 'T' to denote either free or twisted. The most easily created twists are 2/1T and 4/1T. When practising the technique it is best to use fairly thick strands; finer gauges can be used later. You will need something around which to loop your thread as you twist (see Figs B2, B3, and B4). If possible, find a spot where you can screw in a cup-hook and leave it for future use. Whatever you use it must be unmoving and thin. To create a 2/1T:

1 Cut a length of floss about 90cm (3ft) long.

2 Catch it around the hook and even up the ends. Holding both ends in your left hand, create a loop with your right hand and drop the loop over the hook. Move one strand around the hook so that a single strand is coming from each side.

3 Take the strand coming from the right of the hook and hold it against the

heel of the right hand with the fingertips of the left. Roll the strand up the right hand, catch it at the fingertips and repeat.

4 Release the tension on about a third of the strand. The loop formed should be about 3mm (⅛in) across.

5 Pull the twisted strand to one side and tape it to a firm object to prevent it from unwinding. Repeat steps 3 and 4 above with the other strand, twisting it in the same direction. You have now *undertwisted* your thread.

6 Bringing the two twisted strands together, make the first motion of a simple knot, by passing one end over the other. Hold the ends of both strands against the heel of the left hand with the right fingertips and roll the strands up the left hand. Check the tension by repeating step 4 above, but this time the reverse twist should mean that the thread will not form a loop. If the ply is too loose (ie, the thread is not holding together) apply a further reverse twist. The thread is now *overtwisted* and ready to use.

To create a 4/1T, the same procedure is followed, substituting a pair of strands on either side of the hook for the single strand used in a 2/1T.

For a 3/1T it is necessary to split one of the single strands in half in order that you can twist one and a half strands on either side of the hook.

USING BLENDING FILAMENTS

Blending filaments (fine specialist threads containing cellophane or metallic strands) are intended to be used in conjunction with other threads to highlight and emphasize features. They can either be used loosely in a 2/1F thread, making up half the thickness of the thread, more subtly as a smaller percentage of a 3/1F or 4/1F, or twisted into a 2/1T, 3/1T or 4/1T, making a much more compact thread. To use them in twisted threads, follow the procedures set out above, substituting the blending filament for as many strands of the finished thread as you require.

They may also be split down into their essential elements, giving the opportunity of including a fine cellophane strand alone with floss silk, or twisted into a very narrow 2/1T.

TRANSLATING YOUR SKETCHES

Whether you are working from your own sketch, from a design suggested by the drawings in this book, or from a photograph or pre-prepared design, the first step is to transfer the pattern from paper to fabric. It is important to remember that every line which is transferred on to your background fabric is there permanently, and must therefore be covered by embroidery. Very fine details should be omitted from the

Fig B5 ▽
When planning your design, you may like to use the classical 'perfect dimension' of 16:9, on which the Parthenon was based. Seen empty, the resulting rectangle seems elongated, but the dimension becomes easily filled and is strangely harmonious to the human eye. It can be used landscape or portrait

transfer process, as fine embroidery would not be heavy enough to disguise the transferred line. Such fine detail must be worked freehand at a later date.

For transferring a design to fabric you will need:

- Tracing paper
- A large piece of firm cardboard (or wooden drawing board)
- Straight pins (drawing pins)
- Dull pencil, or other stylus
- Ruler
- Dressmaker's carbon paper (dressmaker's tracing paper)
- A flat, smooth table
- Background fabric (remember to leave a large border around your work for mounting)

Tracing paper is available in various weights. A good weight is approximately 90gsm, but you may need to undertake a little trial and error before you find the right weight for your chosen fabric.

DO NOT be tempted to use a typewriter carbon paper. The carbon will rub off on the fabric and is very difficult to remove. Dressmaker's carbon paper (or dressmaker's tracing paper) which is available in most fabric and embroidery stores and haberdashery departments is designed specifically for our purposes. It can usually be bought in packets of assorted colours and has a hard, waxy finish.

METHOD

1 Make a tracing of the chosen design. Place a sheet of tracing paper (this may have to be cut to size) over the pattern and carefully draw over each line with a lead pencil. In any large areas of the design which will be entirely covered by embroidery, you may wish to indicate the direction of stitching by shading. Check that you have traced all the required information (minus fine detail) before removing the paper from the design.

2 Place the cardboard on a flat surface, and lay your fabric out on it. If you use a wooden drawing board make sure that it is padded with several sheets of lining paper as this is necessary to produce a smooth, even line. Carefully position the traced design over the fabric, making sure that the 'north/south' alignment of the design is in line with the weave of the fabric. If the design is to be centred, use a ruler to find the midpoint. Pin the design to the fabric and into the board at the four corners, using the drawing pins.

Do not forget the importance of leaving a good sized border around your work, for effect as well as mounting. Your design may suddenly look very small on a large expanse of fabric, but this is only an illusion.

Fig B6 ▽
The carbon paper, shown partly hatched, is interleaved carefully between the background fabric and the design paper

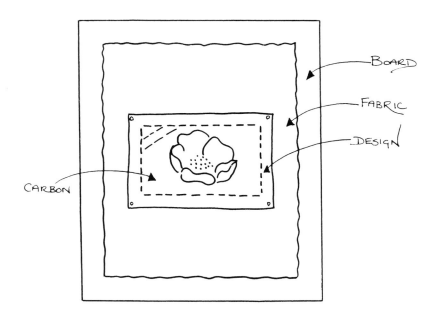

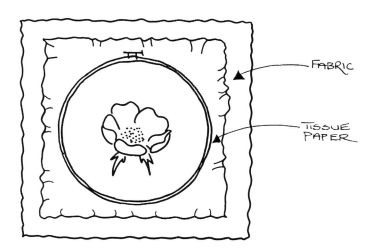

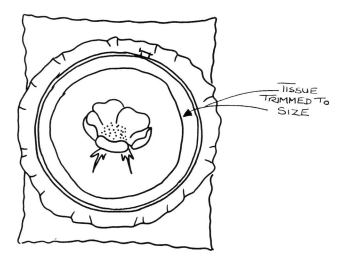

3 Choose a sheet of carbon paper in a colour which contrasts to your fabric. (White 'chalked' carbon paper will rub off as work progresses, so beginners may prefer to use the more waxy yellow or orange carbon paper on dark fabrics.)

Slip the carbon, colour side down, between the tracing and the fabric, removing one of the corner pins to do so. Replace the pin. Do not pin through the carbon paper. Using your pencil (your pencil should be dull, as a sharp pencil applying a hard pressure to the tracing paper will damage it) trace a few lines of the design. Remove one of the pins, raise one corner of the tracing and the carbon and check the impression. If the result is too heavy, apply slightly less pressure, if it is too light, a little more pressure. Replace the sheets and the pin and trace the whole of the design through on to the fabric. Take care not to smudge the carbon by resting your hand on top of the tracing while working, and do not let the pencil mark the fabric.

4 Remove the carbon and all but two of the top pins and check that all the design is transferred before removing the tracing.

PREPARING THE EMBROIDERY
There are various methods of 'dressing' a tambour frame and you should chose that one that suits you best. The procedure set out below has the advantage of not adding any weight to a hand-held frame and it may be used on all types and sizes of tambour frames.

1 Lay the inner ring of the tambour on a flat, clean surface.

2 Over this, place a sheet of tissue paper. If a large frame is used (ie larger than the individual sheets of paper) cut the tissue into wide strips and stick them loosely to the ring using double-sided sticky tape.

3 Position the fabric over this, and put a second sheet of tissue paper over both. If a large frame is used, cut wide strips of the paper and lay them around the edges of the work.

4 Position the outer ring of the frame over the whole ensemble and press down smoothly but firmly. If using a keyed frame, tighten the screw to the appropriate tension.

Fig B7 (above left) △
The tissue paper lies on top of the fabric, the upper ring of the frame ready to hold the two together. The design would be hidden beneath the tissue at this stage; it is shown here to indicate its position within the frame

Fig B8 (above right) △
Once mated with its lower counterparts, the frame becomes whole, sandwiching two layers of tissue and fabric. The tissue is then cut away top and bottom to reveal the design, and conveniently trimmed around the outside of the ring for ease of handling

5 Cut away the tissue paper to reveal the design beneath. Turn the frame over and cut away the tissue paper at the back to reveal the underside of the work. The remaining paper will protect the edges and avoid leaving a 'ring' around your finished work.

WORKING LARGE CANVASES

From time to time you may wish to work an embroidery which is too large to fit even a free-standing quilter's tambour frame. Special procedures must be followed in these cases, and great care taken that in moving the embroidery within the frame no damage is caused to the embroidery already completed, and no smudges created in the transferred design. Using a large cartoon as an example (Fig B9), it is clear that only approximately half the design will comfortably fit the frame at any one time.

1 Decide which section of the embroidery you wish to work first. (If you are right handed this will be the left-hand section and vice versa if you are left handed.) Cover the inner ring of the frame with tissue paper as described above and lay the appropriate section of the fabric in position.

2 Place a second sheet of tissue paper over the fabric (as above) but where the transferred design is to be held between the rings of the frame place an extra couple of sheets as added padding.

3 Position the outer ring with the key (if any) at the top, press down and tighten as before.

4 Cut away the excess tissue paper to reveal the section to be worked (similarly on the reverse).

Fig B9 ▽
The work, 62 x 26cm (24½ x 10in), is to be mounted on a backing board of 72 x 36cm (28½ x 14in), indicated by the outer line. Enough fabric must also be allowed for folding under and turning back (see Figs B13 and B14). Worked on a free-standing tambour frame 56cm (22in) across, it is important that the 'cut off' line (shown broken) should pass through an area containing as little activity as possible, allowing the two areas to be worked independently and merged as smoothly as possible

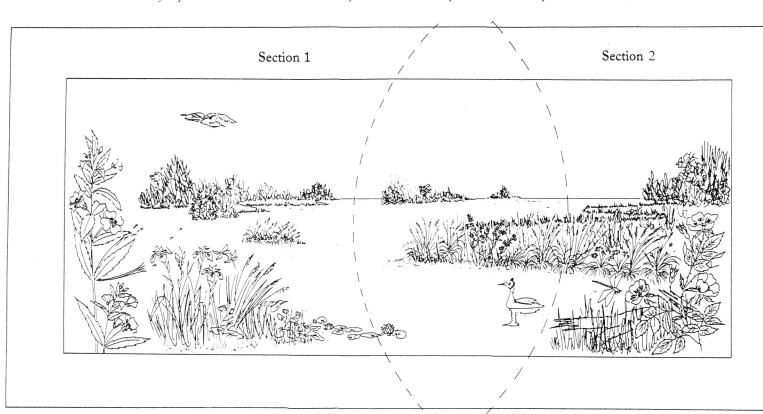

Section 1   Section 2

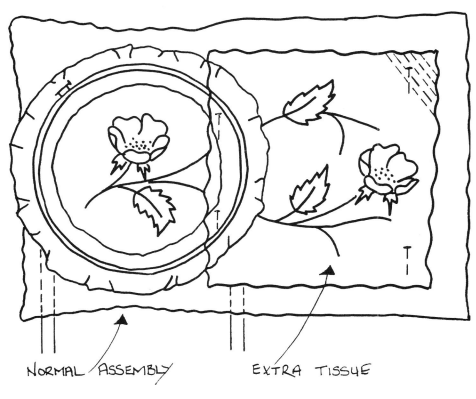

NORMAL ASSEMBLY   EXTRA TISSUE

◁ *Fig B10*
If possible, lay even a free-standing frame flat to achieve this assembly. The additional tissue paper, shown partly hatched, is pinned loosely over the section of the design to be protected

5 Pin a large sheet of tissue paper to the fabric, extending sideways to protect the design still outside the frame. Roll up the fabric with the tissue paper inside to protect the transfer and tape it to the edge of the frame.

6 When the first section of the embroidery has been completed, dismantle the frame and repeat the procedure above. Take particular care when assembling the rings positioned over embroidery already worked, and at step 5 use several sheets of tissue paper to pad out and protect the fabric to be rolled up as this time it will include the embroidery itself!

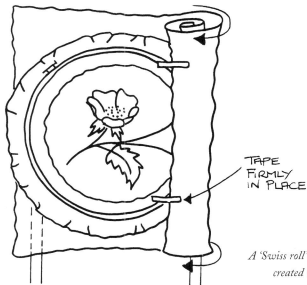

TAPE FIRMLY IN PLACE

◁ *Fig B11*
A 'Swiss roll' of fabric and tissue paper is created and taped to the frame

WORKING A PAIR OF EMBROIDERIES
It is possible to economize on fabric, while still enjoying the flexibility of a free-standing frame, by working a pair of small embroideries at the same time on one frame. During the transfer process position the designs as shown in Fig B12. If you are left handed they will be mirrored. Make sure that you leave enough room between the two for them to be separated when work is complete and remember this must allow for the

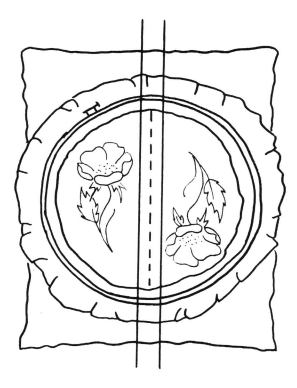

Fig B12 △

If two embroideries are to be worked on a single frame, remember to allow enough fabric between the pair for mounting

border around the work necessary for mounting etc. Position the key (if any) away from either of the designs.

At all times when not in use your frame and its precious contents should be covered and kept clean. Work on pale fabric, in particular, is vulnerable to the least speck of dirt. Always wash your hands before beginning to embroider and throw a cover over your frame if you leave it unattended – particularly if you are working outdoors!

PRESENTATION

Mounting

For mounting, you will need:

- Hardboard (or very stiff cardboard) cut to the size of the finished work (remember to make this big enough for the framing, and smooth off the edges thoroughly)
- Acid-free cartridge paper cut to the same size, white for work on a pale ground, black for work on black
- Clear sticky tape
- Fabric scissors
- Two large-eyed needles
- Lacing thread (mercerized cotton, or similar thread which will not stretch)
- Iron and ironing board

Method

1 Press the embroidery on the wrong side, without steam (after checking the manufacturer's instructions for fabric and thread).

2 Using a small amount of sticky tape, secure the cartridge paper to the surface of the board.

3 Position the embroidery right side up over the covered board, and leaving a margin of at least 4cm (1½in) cut the fabric to size. Leave a larger margin for larger pieces of work or for heavy fabric.

4 Carefully, and without shifting the position of the embroidery in relation to the board, turn the whole ensemble over so that the embroidery is face down, with the board on top of it. Make sure you are working on a clean surface.

5 Cut a long but manageable piece of lacing thread, and thread a needle at each end of the thread, with two 'tails' of similar length.

6 Fold the two sides of the fabric to the centre of the board.

7 Working from the top, insert a needle on either side and lace the two sides of the fabric together corset

fashion until you reach the bottom. If you run out of lacing thread, simply tie the thread off and begin again with more thread.

8 Fold the top and bottom of the fabric towards the centre and repeat the lacing process. It takes a little practice to achieve perfect tension. Do not over-tighten the laces as they may break, or rip the fabric, but do not be afraid of creating a reasonable pull on the work as only in this way will the original tension of the

fabric on the tambour be re-created. Always tie off the ends of the lacing thread with firm, non-slip knots, and snip off any extra thread which is left.

MOUNTING LARGE EMBROIDERIES
Particular care must be taken when preparing a large embroidery for mounting. The larger the canvas, the greater the tension which may be needed to keep it taut on its backing board. Before lacing, therefore, the edges of the work should be turned

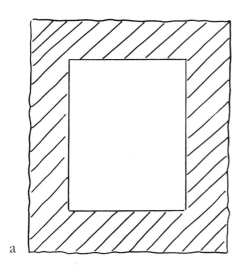

a

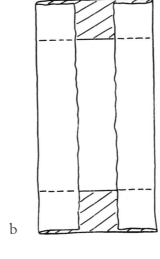

b

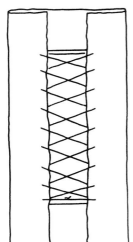

c

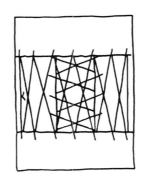

d

◁ Fig B13
Mounting the embroidery:
a Embroidery is placed face down, backing board positioned on top
b The outer sides of the fabric are folded in
c They are laced, corset fashion
d The top and bottom edges of the fabric are treated similarly

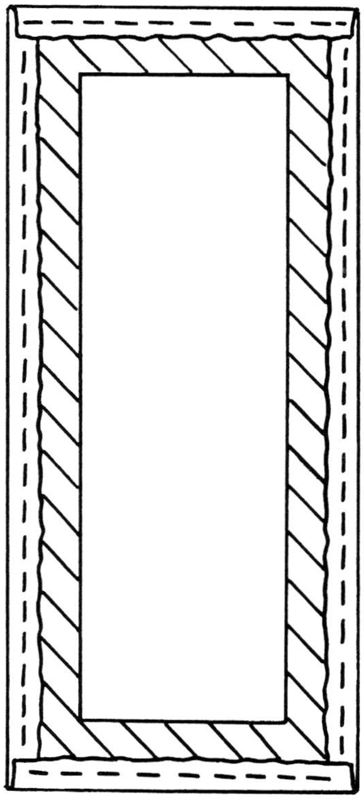

Fig B14 ▷
With the embroidery face down and the board in position, turn back a 'hem' of fabric and tack in position. When lacing the work in place stitch through both layers of the hem for added strength when mounting a large or oddly proportioned piece

back to allow the lacing thread to pass through two thicknesses of fabric. When put under pressure the fabric will be less likely to tear.

When mounting a long, narrow embroidery (such as that featured in Fig B9) lace whichever dimension is the greater first. Do not pull the lacing too tight, as even a rigid backing board, such as hardboard, will bow if put under excessive tension.

Circular or Oval Mounts

Repeat steps 1 to 4 under 'Method' on page 138, but leave a slightly larger border of fabric around the backing board.

5 Cut a piece of lacing thread the length of the circumference of the circle of fabric and thread a single large-eyed needle.

6 Work a line of running stitch approximately 3 or 4cm (1–1½in) inside the edge of the fabric, leaving the ends of the lacing thread on the right side of the embroidery.

7 Check that the design is still centrally located and draw up the running stitches. Tie off the thread and snip off the excess.

8 The pleats of fabric which have been formed by drawing up the lacing thread will be standing proud. Using an iron at the correct temperature press them firmly all in one direction.

Miniatures

The basic process for mounting miniatures is similar to that described above for either straight-edged, circular or oval work. However, remember that your frame will be a great deal smaller, not only in width and height, but also in depth (ie, rebate; see 'Framing' below). The margin of fabric to be turned back, while wide enough to safely accept the lacing thread, should be as narrow as possible to avoid bulk; similarly the lacing thread itself. It should not be necessary to exert great tension on a very small piece, as the embroidery itself will be very light.

It is particularly important to check that there are no specks of dust, fluff or tiny pieces of silk adhering to the front of a miniature before framing. Something the size of a pinhead, which might be overlooked on a larger piece, will assume major proportions on a study only two inches high. It is a good idea always to make a careful inspection of the front of the work, whatever its size, before moving on to the final stage or presentation.

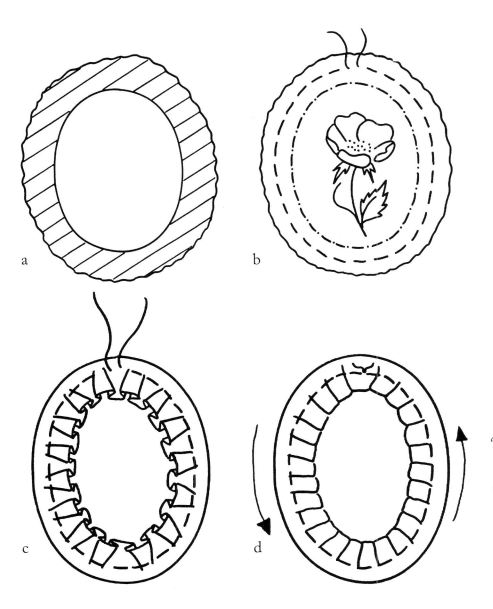

◁ *Fig B15*
a Embroidery face down, the oval mounting board is placed on top
b Face up (position of mounting board indicated by dot/dash line) running stitches are worked around the edge of the fabric
c Draw up the running stitches to form a series of pleats
d Press all the pleats in one direction to reduce bulk

FRAMING

The choice of frame is a personal matter, but always be prepared to take professional advice, as framing can make or mar a picture. On a practical level, the rebate on any frame must be deep enough to accommodate the mounted work, the window mount required to lift the glass from the work (essential if beads etc have been used), the glass and a sheet of cardboard holding the ensemble together.

Avoid hanging work immediately above radiators or fireplaces, and avoid bathrooms and kitchens. No picture should be hung in direct prolonged sunlight. However, to be seen to their best advantage, embroideries need a good level of lighting and ordinary daylight will do little harm. A small spotlight positioned so that it illuminates the work from above will bring it to life, especially in the evenings. Take a little time to achieve the most effective angle of lighting.

SELECT BIBLIOGRAPHY

BOOKS

Aeschylus (translated by Ted Hughes), *The Oresteia* (Faber and Faber, 1999)

Browning, Robert, *My Last Duchess* from The School Book of English Verse (Macmillan & Co., 1938)

Cornwall, Barry, *English Songs and Other Poems,* from The Penny Magazine (Charles Knight, July 1892)

Hawthorne, Nathaniel, *The Scarlet Letter* (Everyman Edition, No.122, 1965)

Herbert, Frank, *Dune* (Victor Gollancz, 1966)

Ingoldsby, Thomas, *The Jackdaw of Rheims,* from The School Book of English Verse (Macmillan & Co., 1938)

Kingsley, Charles, *The Water Babies* (Everyman Edition, No.277, 1936)

Longfellow, Henry Wadsworth, *Autumn,* from Favourite Verse (Parragon, 1999)

Maxwell, Gavin, *Ring of Bright Water* (Longman Green & Co., 1960)

McCollough, Coleen, *The Thorn Birds* (Macdonald and Jane, 1977)

Peake, Meryvn, *Gormenghast* (Vintage, 1999)

Poe, Edgar Allen, *The Masque of the Red Death,* from Tales of Mystery and Imagination (Oldhams Press, c. 1950)

Stevens, Helen M., *The Embroiderer's Countryside* (David and Charles, 1992)

   The Embroiderer's Country Album (David and Charles, 1994)

   The Timeless Art of Embroidery (David and Charles, 1997)

   The Myth and Magic of Embroidery (David and Charles, 1999)

   Helen M. Stevens' Embroidered Flowers (David and Charles, 2000)

   Helen M. Stevens' Embroidered Butterflies (David and Charles, 2001)

Tolkein, J.R.R., *The Lord of the Rings* (George Allen & Unwin, 1966)

MUSIC

Bowie, David, *Space Oddity* (Phillips, 1969)

Coward, Noel, *Poor Little Rich Girl,* from 'Noel Coward in Las Vegas' (CBS, 1966)

Warren, Harry and Dubin, Al, *The Lullaby of Broadway,* from Gold Diggers of 1935 (Warner Bros., 1935)

ACKNOWLEDGMENTS

As ever, my thanks are due to a number of people who were supportive in the preparation of this book, especially clients who kindly allowed their pictures to be reproduced, including plate numbers:

1 Gail Roche; 7 Linda Scott; 9 & 32 Mrs Sheila Wakerley; 10 & 63 Tony Towl; 17, 60 & 61 Mrs Debbie Brodie; 18 & 19 Cynthia Atkins; 23 Master James Plumb; 24 Mrs J. Taylor Balls; 26 & 27 Mrs Helen Rae; 34 Elizabeth Hopewell; 36 Mrs Aurea F. Stevens; 40 Sue Peck; 42 Mr and Mrs Roughton; 44 Linda Clements; 54 Pam Crossley; 64 Mrs C.B. Freeman; 69 Irene Izzard; 70 Laura Brownsea; 73 Mrs E. Coryn.

Plate 28 first appeared in *Needlecraft* magazine, Future Publishing.

Plate 14 first appeared in *Stitches* magazine, Embroiderers' Guild Publishing.

Plate 40 is available as a pure silk kit from Pipers Specialist Silks – see Suppliers.

I am also grateful to Nigel Salmon for his tireless efforts in photographing each piece to its best advantage, and to Cheryl Brown and the team at David and Charles for their back-up, and to my parents for helping in a hundred and one little ways.

This book is also for Steve, who was there when my world changed.